# TABLE OF CONTENTS

Page

# ACRONYMS

BiH          Bosnia and Herzegovina

U.S.         United States

UN          United Nations

# CHAPTER 1

# INTRODUCTION

The international community is struggling with a problem. That problem is the instability caused by weak, failed, or failing states. What kind of policy can the United States and the international community pursue which increases the likelihood that stability arises in failed and failing states? Current efforts by the international community to shore up instability are done through state-building activities. Unfortunately, the primary vehicle for this activity is democratization. This process has an abysmal success rate.

So what is driving this inquiry? I want to know what the international community is overlooking that routinely leads it to fail in the creation of stable state systems through democratization during state-building. Is there a means to improve the operational and planning processes which will help the international community mitigate previous failures in future endeavors? Decision makers whose intent is to foster stability in other states via state-building should prioritize the cultivation of indigenous systems (economic, judicial, social, and security) over externally-imposed systems and stability over democratization.

In order to assess these questions, I use a case study methodology. I analyze four states and use Craig Parsons's Institutional causal logic. Using Parsons's Institutional causal logic helps identify the path dependency of actions by international actors and the unintended consequences therein. An answer to stability may lie in those unintended consequences.

Through the case studies, two significant findings and two themes emerge. The main findings are that the international community routinely disregards the development of indigenous institutions and capabilities in lieu of their own systems and that the indigenous population is not an active part of the planning and execution process of state-building. These ideas are closely related. Two themes also arose. The first is the idea that each country's problems are the result of internal rather than external strife. State-building, as discussed in this paper, does not address these underlying grievances. The second theme is that foreign aid creates negative consequences for the recipient state in terms of social and economic development. Collectively, the themes and main findings prevent the establishment of stable economic systems because the emphasis in state-building is political or regime change without due consideration of the unintended consequences that democratization and the imposition of foreign systems may have on the recipient state.

This project is significant because it provides an alternative perspective for policy makers to consider as they begin planning the next state-building endeavor. Current processes plans do not produce the intended results, so there must be another way to approach each situation. My theory is meant to be a guideline for future endeavors. As an international community, we have to get better at state-building. Stability is good enough as a starting point when addressing international security concerns. Democracy promotion should not be forced. Strengthening indigenous systems and helping to organize functioning systems appropriate for the environment could provide the stability sought by the international community.

The questions and findings presented here are subject to debate. The work is rudimentary, but identifies a fundamentally important concept that affects international security and our way of life. It is my intention to continue researching this topic, to broaden the case studies, provide more rigorous analysis, test the theory against competing hypotheses, and best identify the key causes which prevent stability formation after state-building efforts.

The four countries are broken up into two categories. First, I look at Somalia and East Timor as examples where the leading action by the international community was to externally impose systems over indigenous development. Second, Haiti and Bosnia and Herzegovina (BiH) are assessed as states where the international community's action was democratization over stability development. I choose these four countries because they are all relevant to U.S. interests. Our primary interests with weak, failed, and failing states reside in the area of security and humanitarian causes. Security concerns emanating from weak, failing, and failed states was specifically mentioned in the 2012 U.S. National Security Strategy and in previous versions since 2002.

Somalia has been the top failed state according to Foreign Policy's Failed State Index since 2008. It has been in the top 10 since 2005. Somali pirates, an unintended consequence of the ability to supplant a stable state system, are a significant security threat to international interests. U.S. resources are expended daily to address the situation in Somalia.

Similarly, East Timor, a Pacific island northwest of Australia, is a hotbed of insurgent activity and has the potential to great greater instability in the region. This could affect our efforts in nearby states of the Philippines, Indonesia, and Malaysia. East

Timor is high on the list of failed states, but consistently place 20th. When the international community pulled out of East Timor in 2005, it was considered the poster-child of a successful state-building endeavor. So what when wrong?

Haiti is a compound and complex environment. Our interests may not be obvious. The island does not have any significant resources, nor is it a major trading partner. U.S. interests relate to its physical proximity. The paper discusses that instability is not localized; it has to potential to expand beyond state boundaries–effecting regional and international activity. A stable Haiti is good for the U.S. The situation is compounded because of the profound humanitarian needs on the island. Due to its geographic location, Haiti is also prone to natural disasters such as earthquakes and hurricanes. This adds additional challenges that a state like BiH need not contend.

BiH became a huge bleep on the radar in 1995. To prevent further genocide, the international community rushed in following the Srebrenica massacre after moderately observing the environment for three years. Stability of the former Yugoslavian states was a risk, and BiH seemed to be the lead domino. U.S. interests remain because of humanitarian concerns that violence may erupt again.

Three of the four states were former colonies. BiH is the exception. However, it was similarly controlled by an external entity for decades as part of the former Yugoslavia, under Marshal Josef Tito. The main difference is the level to which the colonial power or Tito allowed the indigenous population to participate in government. Under colonial rule, indigenous populations operated only at very low levels within the governing structure, and directly supervised by a colonial. In contrast, in the Former

Yugoslavia, indigenous populations operated at all levels in the government. They were also over watch, but by the Communist Party whose members were local citizens.

Developing my theory requires a literature review on state-building, democracy, democratic promotion, intervention, political transitions, and stability. Chapter 2 presents a broad discussion of these topics. State-building and nation-building are mature fields of study. However, there is little discussion as to why state-building is rigorously paired with democratic promotion. If stability is the first priority, even non-democratic governance supporting stable system could be acceptable. Too often the powerful western states like the U.S. and the United Nations (UN) promote democracy over stability at the expense of the recipient state. Reasons for a democratic promotion priority are many, but include the influence of the Democratic Peace Theory and experiences during the Cold War. As a result, literature discussing state-building apart from democratization is limited.

In chapter 3, I use a case-study methodology and Parsons's typology of causal logics to assess the foreign imposition in lieu of developing indigenous capabilities and democratization over stability. Limitations in the study include focusing on Parsons's institutional causal logic knowing that there may other causal logics at play. Additionally, the relatively short time period of eleven-years[1] does not allow international community time to incorporate changes and lessons from past experiences into future endeavors. Four cases may be seen as a weakness, as can my assumptions that the indigenous population will reject externally imposed systems that do not inculcate ideas and norms

---

[1]The eleven-year period marks the beginning of the first intervention in 1991 to the last intervention beginning in 2002. Efforts continue in all four states to some degree.

of the population and culture and that the international community is more concerned with pushing their own agendas, thereby disregarding the needs of the recipient state. Strengths of the work include the eleven-period duration. The short timeframe of study is also a strength because the period clearly identifies patterns of international behavior during the height of state-building endeavors. That this paper provides an alternate perspective for further research and debate is important. My theory creates a guideline. It is not meant to be a cookie-cutter solution to complex problems; observations are at the macro level and cannot incorporate the challenges presented by individuals or groups. People are unpredictable.

Chapter 4 presents the four case studies and my findings. Parsons's institutional causal logic is informative in identifying actions and the related unintended consequences and useful for extracting discussion points which form my theory. Somalia and East Timor are used to review possible effects of externally imposing systems in lieu of developing indigenous ones. State building activity began in Somalia in 1992. Civil war broke out when despot, General Siad Barre, was ousted. The land is a community of tribes, strong historical ties and no respect for outsiders or other tribes. It is a closed system. Under a UN mandate, the U.S. went into Mogadishu to support humanitarian efforts, but transitioned to assist in controlling tribal warfare in the city. They were unable to do so and became targets for their efforts. They also tried to instill democratic institutions and associated systems which are foreign to Somalis and counter their culture and historical understanding of governance and justice. U.S. troops pulled out in 1994 and the second UN mission ended in 1995. Actions and unintended consequences include the imposition of a central government which neglected the long-held tribal system and did not address power distribution. This caused greater conflict among the warring

powers as they sought control of state resources. Another action was the Disarmament,

Demobilitization, and Reintegration program. Since the U.S. and UN mission were

unable to establish a strong government, its own weakness continued working against it.

Promises made under the program never materialized and created a new level of

disenfranchisement among the Somalis that agreed to participate in the program. These

individuals turned to gangs and crime, often supported by tribal war lords. A third action

is that of foreign aid. The distribution of aid was inconsistent and rarely reached the

intended recipients. What aid did get through was used by warlords to increase their

power. The continuing humanitarian issues creates a cycle for more aid. It also inhibits

domestic development because of the amount of foreign aid available.

In East Timor, the UN created a Transitional government in 2002 and departed in

2005 declaring success. The state was in ruins after Indonesian soldiers raze the country

when they occupation ended. Portugal, its colonial ruler, lets the land fall to the way-side.

When the UN arrives, there are existing political elites but they have no infrastructure or

capital. The leading political factions or parties struggle for dominance and control of the

state. Underlying tensions never eased more where they addressed and indigenous

population was not nurtured for their new place as a free state. The study identified two

actions which lead to unintended consequences. First the exclusion of the local

population from senior and significant levels in the Transitional government and the

planning process in general. This created distrust among the Timorese toward the UN

officers. It also failed to develop the indigenous population for self-rule. This leads to the

second action of UN malevolence. UN officer disregard for the Timorese and their capabilities prevents development. Power struggles among UN officers at all level prevented infrastructure development. These limitations add to population unrest. Findings to the topic of externally imposed systems over indigenous identify a lack of connection and coordination with the local population and a disregard for local institutions, along with domestic capability and resilience.

The second category is democratization over stability as a focus of the state-building activity. The U.S. intervened in Haiti in 1994 after the elected president was ousted from power by a military coup. The U.S. facilitated the return of President Aristide and supported his government. Significant humanitarian operations were also present. The U.S. ended its mission without providing development to the economy or other institutions outside of the presidency. Aristide was ousted again in 2004, and the U.S. returned to put him back in power. Haiti is a democracy in name, but not in practice. The U.S. blindly supported the name of democracy regardless of the actions of the president, which were extractive in nature. Aristide and his party *Lavalas*, actively counter democratic development because it is in their interests. This is common among political elites with extractive policies and economies. Democracies threaten their power base and therefore the state cannot expand. Actions of interest found in this case start with the reinforcement of the ousted President. Aristide's reinstallment empowered corrupt officials and stifles development, as noted above. A second action is the lack political and economic development. The state was already failed, so it needed infusions in many areas to expand. Without indigenous development in many sectors, growth could not materialize. Development includes education. There was no plan to educate the population on what democracy is and what it can mean to the citizen. The last action is

8

donor aid, once again. In Haiti, the government failed to monitor and control aid. The result was lack of desire to build domestic industry because they can get the free stuff. It also nearly destroyed domestic textile and grain markets because lack of governmental oversight.

The last case is BiH. It was part of the former Yugoslavia and hosted 1984 Winter Olympics in Sarajevo. Ethnic cleansing among all parties–Serbs, Croats, and Bosniacs (Muslims) occurred during the civil war which began in 1992. Hostilities date back for ages. War rhetoric uses past losses to justify actions against others. The state has three unique cultures but they are the same people. In terms of politics, Croats are most moderate with the Bosniacs second–although they cry injustice despite significant support of the international community; Serbs want an independent state. The 1995 Dayton Peace Accord is a source of malcontent and mismanagement by UN officials to create a stable state. Two actions of interests here begin with the election process. The elections reinforce ethnic cleavages. Real power at the national level, resides in the Office of the High Representative, a UN office, regardless of who is elected. Absolute control over indigenous populations does not create strength or confidence in the system or the elected officials. Corruption remains rampant, especially at local levels. Findings in the category of democratization over stability identifies non-inclusion of indigenous population; disregard for local institutions, capacity and resiliency of the population; no political or democratic education; and that foreign aid without planning and management hinder economic and political growth and development.

The theory I present is a guide for decision makers. I conclude that policymakers should prioritize the cultivation of indigenous capabilities and stability by attending to indigenous officials, populations, and systems from the local to national levels. This theory has implications for policymakers considering state-building efforts as a way to increase their respective state's security. State stability is directly related to security issues that may arise from absentee or ill-governed states. Concerns include creating permissive environments for international terrorists training and organization to trade routes for international criminal activity. Instability can affect regional and international actors due to various levels of interdependence. Conflict containment, shoring up weak and failing states, and salvaging failed states are necessary activities to bring about secure, stable states. Efforts in state-building reflect these concerns. Therefore, emphasis on democratic promotion and imposition of external systems may not be the best plan. Answers to stability can be found within the state itself.

# CHAPTER 2

## LITERATURE REVIEW

Literature on state-building and democracy is well developed in political science. Discussions began post World War I; made a large leap after World War II and the decolonization period in the 1950s and 1960s. The world braced for new rounds of state-building activity and debate after the Berlin Wall fell in 1989 and the 1991 collapse of both the Socialist Republic of Yugoslavia and the Union of Soviet Socialist Republics.

Dynamic changes in the international scene lead to shifts in state-building literature. Pre-Cold War literature showed a propensity for incorporating domestic systems; scholars and practitioners saw incorporation as necessary for state building success (Watson 2005). Likely, the experiences of rebuilding Germany and Japan influenced attitudes that domestic resourcing would create stable states. However, many scholars caution referring back to Germany and Japan because the their domestic conditions are significantly different from post-colonial and post-Cold War states. Specifically, Germany and Japan were militarily defeated nations, infrastructure was significantly destroyed, insurgent or rebel groups were quickly quelled; they had no memories of colonization, but did have homogenous populations, and a history of successful social, economic, and bureaucratic structures (Dixon 2011, 2; Dobbins 2006, 225; Somit and Peterson 2005, 42). Today, scholars like David Chandler note that current UN interactions with indigenous parites demonstrate distrust toward the local population and their political solutions, assuming anying indigenous to be problematic (Chandler 2007, 71). Levels of distrust are more apparent the greater the fundamental societal differences are between the interveners and the recipient state.

Despite the maturity of state-building literature and related fields of democracy, security, and stability, a gap remains. Only limited attempts have been made to separate state-building and democracy. Such discussions are often hidden in broader arguments and therefore have not received due attention. Literature overlooks state-building as a separate activity from democratic promotion. To build my theory, I must first discuss the literature and gap in more detail.

## History of State-Building

Western states such as the U.S., United Kingdom, and France have participated in state building for hundreds of years as part of empire expansion and colonization (Acemoglu and Robinson 2012). Tens of new states emerged after World War II and decolonization. Democratization and externally imposed systems were the norm during the colonial period and continues into modern times through state-building.

History can provide examples of where democratization and externally imposed systems had positive and negative effects. States like India made the transition from colony to statehood rather well; whereas others, Pakistan for example, did not (Sutton 2006, 44). Pakistan was an area of the Indian British colony. Partitioned in 1947, India and Pakistan inherited the same government structures from Britain. Both states retained elements of the British structure to varying degrees (Paine 2010, 17-18; Wolpert 2004, 360). India used the residual systems as a base as they made incremental changes that better matched Indian norms and ideas. Their success is a positive example of the effects of externally imposing systems and democratization. Pakistan, on the other hand, resisted more of the structures after their strongest leader, Muhammad Ali Jinnah, died in 1948 (Read and Fisher 1997, 472). New leaders found British laws to compromise some of the

Muslim ways they wished to incorporate. Pakistan also had a challenge with the local population. All members of the new government were from New Delhi, not Islamabad, Pakistan's new capital city. The new political elite displaced the former tribal elites in the area. Displacement and power shifts caused trust and legitimacy issues among the population toward the new political elites. Effects of the imposition of the new Pakistani government in Islamabad can be seen as a micro example of what can go badly with foreign imposition of systems. Pakistan, unable to coalesce around foreign systems and leaders, has increasingly become a threat to regional and international security.

Years of practicing state-building have not made the U.S. or international organizations like the UN quantifiable experts who can guarantee results. Jeffery Pickering and Mark Peceny studied 49 democratic transitions between 1946 and 1996. They found that transitions by military imposition, UN and North Atlantic Treaty Organization intervention had equally poor records in establishing stable states. The U.S. was considered successful in only one endeavor, Panama. Meanwhile, the UN was remotely successful in four of five cases–Cyprus, Mozambique, Honduras, and Nicaragua. Pickering and Peceny accounted the UNs success to the fact that missions were for peacekeeping not peace imposition (Pickering and Peceny 2006). Gregory Dixon argues that when democracies intervene, their mission execution is limited by their own domestic concerns such as public opinion, funding, and leader status within public institutions (Dixon 2011, 3). Cynthia Watson agrees with Dixon, to a point; she claims that limitations are related to the interveners' goals and not the recipient states' needs (Watson 2004, 10).

One can argue that the current preponderance of democratic overtures in state-building is a reflective of Cold War policies. U.S. foreign policy developed in direct response to the spread of communism by the Union of Soviet Socialist Republics. John Owen hypothesizes that foreign impositions on domestic institutions are because the greater power wants to expand their own ideology (Owen 2002, 375). If this premise is accepted, all efforts to stabilize states by western powers are attempts to foster democracy over indigenous desires. Such efforts to countermand communist influence established a dangerous precedent for the modern world with regards to how policymakers view state-building.

Democratic Peace Theory

Another topic to review is the Democratic Peace Theory. In many ways, understanding this theory for the most part explains the current international emphasis of democratic promotion through state-building. The theory, in simplistic terms, suggests that democracies do not go to war with one another. Modifications to this theory add that democracies are less likely to go to war with another democracy because of economic and other interdependencies. To illustrate the democratic peace theory, the following question is often posed. Are there any two states at war that also have McDonalds? If the democratic peace theory holds then one could conclude that more democracies in the world equates to less conflict.

This promise of peace is the exact topic of a December 2005 Op-ed by Secretary of State Condoleezza Rice. Here, she recalled President Bush's second inaugural address in which he promoted the spread of democracy as a cure-all for tyranny. She also pointed out the dangers presented to the world from weak and failing states. Rice's op-ed clearly identifies the U.S. interest in stable state systems. It is also reflective of the UN Secretary General's 2000 appeal to promote democracy in all activities. The U.S. and UN promote democracy, according to Secretary Rice, because of the "undeniable truth that democracy is the only assurance of lasting peace and security between states" (Rice 2005).

## Security

Secretary Rice's comments highlight domestic and international concern for security related to weak, failed, and failing states. Nonetheless, overemphasis on democratic promotion and imposition of foreign systems may not be the best solution for long-term stability and hence greater security. Lisa Chauvet, Paul Collier, and Anke Hoeffler, among other scholars agree that non-intervention in certain circumstances, such as in BiH is a failing on the part of the world leaders (Chauvet et al. 2007, 13). When governments become unable to establish or maintain domestic security, bad things happen. Weak, failed, and failing states often give way to ungoverned spaces. These spaces can become training grounds for domestic and transnational terror groups (S. Kaplan 2008/2009; Piazza 2008; Elden 2007; Barnett 2006). When governments cannot control state power and resources, stronger individuals will do so. Competition of power and resources increases conflict which can expand beyond domestic borders, negatively effecting regional and international security issues.

The annual U.S. National Security Strategy continues to comment on the persistent security and weak states issue and has done so for over a decade. (MERLN 2012). President George W. Bush took highlighted these concerns to the world in a comment post-9/11. His words reflect similar fears of within the international community.

I believe that the United Nations would–could provide the framework necessary to help meet those conditions. It would be a useful function for the United Nations to take over so-called 'nation-building'–I would call it the stabilization of a future government–after our military mission is complete. We'll participate; other countries will participate . . . I've talked to many countries that are interested in making sure that the post-operations Afghanistan is one that is stable, and one that doesn't become yet again a haven for terrorist criminals. (Chesterman 2004, 250)

Kaplan asserts that security of all states teeters on the management of intertwining polity, social, cultural, and environmental realms. Accordingly, where these intersect conflict will ensue and pull the world into an unending cycle of instability (R. Kaplan 1994). Security concerns are a critical link between state-building and democratic promotion. Without security, non-governmental organizations and international organizations will not push forward humanitarian missions. Security is foundational to economic and judicial balance.

Relationship of Democracy and State-Building

State-building has morphed into little more than a vehicle for democratic promotion, even where that was not the original mission intent (von Hippel 2000). Democratic governing systems have gained worldwide strength and momentum since 1918. Leading states often turns to the UN to justify and employ missions to stabilize or rebuild weak, failed, and failing states. UN Secretary-General Kofi Annan's appeal in 2000 directed members to heavily promote democracy, liberal values, and humanitarian rights in all UN missions. Since 2000, UN state-building activities are intentionally designed as democratic state-building efforts.

In a comment related to Secretary Rice's, Karin von Hippel discusses the transition focus shift in state-building and the emphasis on democracy to achieve stability. She states:

16

> Nation building . . . has over the years signified an effort to construct a government that may or may not be democratic, but preferably is stable. Today, (it) normally implies the attempt to create democratic and secure states. Thus democratization efforts are part of the larger and more comprehensive nation-building campaign. (Hippel 2000, 96)

The shift to overt democratization makes it difficult to assess an individual states' capability to shore up indigenous institutions and capabilities that would be more amenable to the local population. It also perpetuates an idea that democracy is the only acceptable form of government and will ensure good governance. However, the notion of good governance under the ruse of democracy is contestable; this is evidenced in the number of partially free democracies listed in the current Freedom in the World report by Freedom House. In the 2012 report, of the states used as case studies, all are considered democracies; three are partially free and one, Somalia, is not free (Freedom House 2012).

One concept in state-building is the ability to legitimize the government. Democratic elections, according to some scholars, is the only means to bring legitimacy to state-building and the domestic government (Fukuyama 2006, 237). However, elections and the transition to democracy can be problematic and hinder stability. Andrea Talentino, among others, challenges the democratic state-building process because they find it creates too much division among the indigenous population and a lack of trust in political leadership (Talentino 2009, 380).

## Challenges in Democracy Promotion

Stability of new democratic states transitions is questionable. Intervention does not ensure that underlying conflicts among warring factions are addressed and resolved. This leaves residual challenges for the newly established government. Others decry the problems of incomplete or partial democracies because they do not live up to the liberal ideals expected by interveners. Nor do incomplete or partial democracies ensure stability (Goldsmith 2008; Samuels 2005; Mansfield and Snyder 2002). During transitions, violence and new conflicts tend to emerge as power shifts among groups. Struggles among political elites, weak governments in transition and fledgling systems combine to increase the likelihood that a state will not withstand the transition (Bueno de Mesquita and Downs 2006; Pickering and Kisangani 2006; Samuels 2005). Francis Fukuyama would agree with these scholars in that real change and stable democracy development takes time and resources. He states that foreigners cannot build states because they come and go over such a short period of time. Democratic state-building requires an "unplanned historical-evolutionary process" for nations to emerge (Fukuyama 2006, 3).

Additional literature addresses concern over the imposition of democracy as state-building from outsiders (Watson 2004; Owen 2002). Fukuyama, Owen, Minxin Pei, and others argue that democracy should develop from within the state. What are the right tools? The U.S. has used military and diplomatic resources. The World Bank is a primary leader in economic development. Other states and institutions what they feel will best address the challenge of state-building. All do so with a democratic, western mindset. Therefore, literature does not discuss the idea of separating state-building activities from democratic promotion. It goes against the ideals of the intervener. Even scholars who question the stability of democratic transitions often support state-building agendas with an end state of a democratic government, free elections, and the implementation of liberal ideals such as women and minority rights. Whatever the imposition, interveners often find that indigenous institutions are often stronger and more resilient than first realized (Watson 2004, 7).

18

## Challenges in State-Building

Where should efforts for state-building focus? When should efforts be employed? How long should the effort continue? Do we want to use hard power through military interventions or soft powers such as sanctions, trade agreements, or other methods presented by the UN or North Atlantic Treaty Organization? How can state-building best establish a safe and secure environment? What monitoring capability or influence will used ensure progress stays on track after the bulk of the international mission departs? These are difficult questions. The more hostile or unstable a state is at the time of intervention influences how the U.S. or other states approach the situation. Experiences with significant resistance or insurgents, as seen in Iraq, forces interveners to emphasize hard power over soft power.

Collier and S.C.M. Paine actively promote financial stability as the path to self-sufficient, stable states (Collier 2011; Paine 2010). According to David Epstein, Robert Bates, Jack Goldstone, Ida Kristensen, and Sharyn O'Halloran, economics appears to play a significant role in stabilizing a state during and after transitions. They found that states transitioning to democracy with a high GDP per capita are more likely to sustain that political system, suggesting increase stability (Epstein et al. 2006). Elements of this argument follow Fukuyama's two-part level of stateness. He acknowledges that the economy helps build stable, competitive states and subsequently democracy. Higher GDP also suggests lower employment. Unemployment within a disaffected population is exploited by terror or insurgent recruiters, which relates back to security issues. In a perfect world, during state-building, this disaffected population would be harnessed as part of the solution.

19

## Stability of Non-Democratic States

While scholars still debate stability of democracies, other government systems are sometimes overlooked. Non-democracies can be stable states. The former Union of Socialist Soviet Republics, China, and the former Yugoslavia were stable states, for a while. The manner in which citizens are managed may be unpalatable to liberal ideals, but the state can be stable nonetheless. Stability is most often challenged when senior leaders transition power.

Authoritarian regimes or monarchies have ruled for decades. Daron Acemoglu and James Robinson note that the explosion of democracies is contrary to political history (Acemoglu and Robinson 2012). By the number, non-democracies outnumber full democracies. In 2010, the Democratic Index published by the Economist Intelligence Unit identified 167 countries in the world. Of those, 25 were considered full democracies, 53 partial democracies, 37 hybrid regimes and 52 authoritarian regimes (Democracy Index 2012). Natasha Ezrow and Erica Frantz find that non-democracies can be quite stable and resilient when they add political parties and legislatures to their structure (Ezrow and Frantz 2011). Like democracies, non-democracies come in slight variations which can account for some stability. Leaders who keep out even the appearance of competing political parties tend to be more problematic in terms of stability. Earlier work from Robert Mundt suggests that defining regime stability by duration of type, non-democracies and partial democracies prove to be more stable than democracies. He concluded that non-democracies are typically replaced by the same whereas new or weak democracies tend to transition back to non-democracies (Mundt 1997).

## The Gap

Democratic promotion has an active place in literature. However, its relationship to state-building has not been examined deeply or recently as discussed here. In his book, *State-building: Governance and World Order in the 21st Century*, Fukuyama introduces his concept of two levels of stateness. The levels of stateness tie directly into the state's ability to cultivate a future democracy in that weak or failing state. The first level is scope which refers to the depth of activity a state controls within its boundaries in matters such as law and order. Second level is efficiency which addresses a state's ability to actually govern and manage economic development. Degrees to which these levels exist in a state are indicative, according to Fukuyama, of how well democracy will prosper (Fukuyama 2004).

Other literature touching closely to concerns about international state-building practices includes Neil Robinson's 2007 and Albert Somit and Steven Peterson's 2005 works. To begin, Somit and Peterson articulate that democracy and state-building are separate concepts (Somit and Peterson 2005, 46). Robinson adds market development into this mix, but warns that simultaneous development may impede development in one or all areas (Robinson 2007, 14).

Chandler's 2007 essay, "The State-building Dilemma: Good Governance or Democratic Government" makes a similar argument to my thesis. He specifically states that "in terms of state-building, democracy and political autonomy are seen to be the end goal, rather than crucial aspects of the process of state-building itself (Chandler 2007, 71). However, he focuses on the ideological shift by international actors on the matter as

21

opposed to my challenge that continuing to operate in support of the two practices precludes the emergence of stability after interveners depart.

Similarly, Owen's 2002 article, "The Foreign Imposition of Domestic Institutions" assesses why states seek to impose their systems on others. He claims that impositions occur when strong states are expanding power and want to spread their own ideology (Owen 2002, 375). Questions in this paper extend from his second reason for imposition–ideological export; in this case, the ideology is democracy. Pei et al. see the principles of state-building as maintaining commitments by the interveners, balancing political legitimacy and reconstruction effectiveness, and planning reconstruction (Pei et al. 2006, 81-82). They discuss Japan as an example of where the interveners managed the balance between politics and development.

Categorizing success in democratization and state-building as a combined effort is difficult. The various organizations or state-building actors have different rubrics for evaluating success. The UN might deem elections with minimal interference as success. Others may regard the length or period of time a state remains conflict free after the international missions ends as a key instrument of measure of success or failure in the state-building endeavor. Roland Paris notes that while all states do not revert to overt violence, often the amount or degree of low-level conflict increases. He continues to suggest that the very efforts to stabilize the state through "- political and economic liberalization -" become the very cause for new violence and instability (Paris 2004, 6).

Chapter 3 presents the methodology, specifically related to Parsons institutional causal logic and topical definitions. Applying this methodology to case studies will lead to a better understanding of the unintended consequences of the two practices in question.

It is important to address how the U.S. and the other world powers might better meet objective for stable states and hence increase security through state-building. Security is a serious issue, as evidence by each state-building activity. The U.S. and other states develop national strategies to combat potential instability caused by weak, failed, and failing states. Nearly all scholars and practitioners agree on the single concept that state-building and democracy promotion is hard work; requiring significant resources and time. Paine notes that "although reconstruction can take place within one generation, even rapid state building and economic development generally takes two or three generations" (Paine 2010, 9).

# CHAPTER 3

## RESEARCH METHODOLOGY

An inductive theory for state-building can aid policymakers pursuing state-building programs, be they new, stalled or misaligned, that seeks stability as the end state. Two practices routinely carried out by international actors during state-building are externally-imposed systems over indigenous systems and the prioritization of building democracies over stability. These practices become evident through the case studies. Employment of these practices has inherent flaws which can unintentionally lead to instability. In order to reduce potential negative consequences of these practices, intervening states need to more actively engage the indigenous populations and focus on stability over democratization. Four case studies follow in chapter 4 for assessment and theory development.

### Methodology

In reviewing the literature, I generated two assumptions. Both refer to the intervener's state of mind. First, the intervener tends to overlook the value in the indigenous systems because of their organizational or national interests, preferences, and comfort levels when developing and instituting democratic systems. Even though indigenous systems may not have the hallmarks of democracy, functioning systems that can be adapted to form a baseline supporting the mission's stabilization goal should be engaged. Second, the indigenous population will reject foreign systems that conflict with their way of life. For change to be sustainable, it must be done in moderation over time. When an exogenous imposition challenges c culture's core beliefs, customs, or traditions it is not likely to be fully embraced. There is a reason sustainable change takes time–and successful state-building cannot be executed on a set timeline.

As a limitation, my assumptions can affect the case study analysis. They may also shed light on a topic not often considered. Either way, the assumptions play their part in conclusions drawn. This state-building theory addresses two issues: development of indigenous systems and stability. Chapter 4 presents four case studies, each identifying the unintended consequences of one of the practices in question. Inductively, I extract elements from case studies of Somalia, East Timor, Haiti, and BiH to build the theory. These elements, unintended consequences caused by actions of the international actors, form the basis of the theory. I use Parsons's typology of causal logic. Parsons identifies four logics: (1) structural–refers to the physical origins like geography; an individual will select the best choice given obstacles and cannot change the physical environment; (2) institutional–refers to formal and informal rules and organizations, and path dependency leading to unintended consequences is the key identifier; (3) ideational– related to culture, values, beliefs, and or communal attributes; and (4) psychological–a perspective that is common to all man, commonly associated with Prospect Theory and Relative Deprivation Theory explaining irrational outcomes (Parsons 2007, 12).

Any theory has its strengths and weaknesses. Using Parsons causal logics can itself be a limiter, because there is often more than a single causal logic is at play. In state-building specifically, breaking down this complicated task solely by Parsons's institutional logic provides grounds to challenge the other influencers. Much like the now oft discussed Arab Spring, no individual causal logic can pinpoint the tipping point or points which led to this phenomenon. The strength in this research is the analysis itself discussed in the chapter 4 summations and in the chapter 5 conclusions. All of the cases initially fall within an eleven-year period (1991-2002), which was the height of state-building efforts by international actors. Issues in these states are still unsettled and the source of much domestic and regional strain and instability. In that time, studies suggested ways to improve organization for this endeavor. As most were rejected as too costly or time consuming, international actors continued to make the same errors, or sought corrections without assessing the underlying reasons. Findings provide guidance to policymakers to help them avoid the unintended consequences in state-building as a result of certain international community practices. Before moving on to chapter 4, it is necessary to provide a few key definitions.

## Definitions

### External Imposition of Systems

I define externally imposed systems as where an intervener forcing systems, government, economic, etc. onto a weak state, where such a system did not exist previously. The system is unfamiliar to the domestic population and may conflict with cultural norms.

### Prioritization of Democracy

Prioritization of democracy refers to the intervening state ignoring the functioning systems and shadow governments and markets which might be useful to state-building development. Such systems are disregarded as they do not fit a democratic model.

## Democracy

Democracy can be defined as "a political system possessing competitive elections plus the protection of political liberties" (Somit and Peterson 2005). This is a fairly simple definition. However, it does not explain the liberal aspect of democracy as the west has come to structure their system. Robert Dahl espouses six principles to describe democracy: elected officials; free, fair, and frequent elections; freedom of expression; access to alternative sources of information; associational autonomy; and inclusive citizenship (Dahl 1998). These principles represent the common form of democracy interveners most often push as state-building.

## State-Building

For the purpose of this paper, there is a distinction between nation-building and state-building. The former refers to the development of people, tribes, and society in general as a community. The later refers to the state institutions that provide public goods, services, and security (Paine 2010). Fukuyama discusses four activities which generally are aspects of state-building: peacekeeping; peace enforcement; postconflict reconstruction or security; and long-term economic and political development or reconstuction of politicy authority (Fukuyama 2006, 232-238). Additionally, he declares that "state-building is the creation of new government institutions and the strengthening of existing ones" (Fukuyama 2004). Alternatively, Simon Chesterman describes state-building as "the extended international involvement that goes beyond traditional peacekeeping and peace building mandates, and is directed at constructing or reconstructing institution of governance capable of providing citizens with physical and economic security" (Chesterman 2004).

27

## Stable State Systems

A stable state is one that is economically self-sufficient, able to provide security and social goods to its citizens and can defend itself from internal or external threats.

## Extractive Practices and Institutions

Extractive practices and institutions are representative of states where power is held in the hands of a few who have broad range of authority over those institutions and no responsibility to the populace. Acemoglu and Robinson discuss extractive and inclusive practices and institutions throughout their book, *Why nations fail*. They argue that states practicing inclusive policies over extractive are more stable and likely to be more successful. They find a correlation between extractive political and economic institutions (Acemoglu and Robinson 2012, 79-83). These practices and institutions can create instability, prevent industrialization, and perpetuate cycles of poverty and abuse of a government over its citizenry.

Paine writes that "resilient state institutions are a function of a strong underlying sense of community" (Paine 2010, 8). This sentiment mirrors that of Rogers Smith in his book *Stories of Peoplehood: The Politics and Morals of Political Membership*. Smith's intent has less to do with nation building, but identifying a means to analyze development and strategies by taking into account the importance of people, their history, culture, and other unique characteristics that inform their decision making process and community development (Smith 2003).

Etzioni makes the argument that development should come from the "periphery to the center." This is a good argument, even though he espouses one of the optium results as development of democratic institutions (Etzioni 2009/2010, 52-53). This is not to say that democracy is not a good form of government, rather stability as an objective does not require immediate political changes toward democracy. Mundt says two pre-conditons are required in a society for democracy to take hold: ideological and social. The first suggests the development of liberal political thought, such as that observed in Western Europe during the enlightenment. Social pre-conditons refer to the societal advancement towards capitalist or individualist markets. If these two preconditions are not met, attempts to promote democracy are likely to create more instability (Mundt 1997). Therefore, it is important to address the needs of the population and facilitate stability with the resources or institutions at hand. Additional tools and resources are brought in as required or requested by the indigenous political leadership. The next chapter explores where democratic and foreign system imposition did not create lasting stability.

# CHAPTER 4

## ANALYSIS

A brief survey of four case studies using Parsons's institutional causal logic suggests state-building actors should be more inclusive of indigenous capabilities when employing state-building missions. Engagement and inclusion must occur at all levels, to include economic, judicial, social, and security. Where developing systems are significantly different from existing structures, intervening states must educate the population as part of the state-building process and attempt to blend new ideas with old.

Stable states are the desired outcome of state-building missions. Stability can be elusive, but it is attainable. I have already discussed the poor grade the international community receives on achieving stability via democratic state-building. My theory is meant to be a tool for policymakers developing or adjusting state-building activity. The intent is to provide an alternative perspective so they do not employ the same practices identified here without due consideration. Actions have consequences, some good, some less good, but thinking through the possibilities as part of initial planning can yield a better result.

I analyze four case studies through Parsons's typological institutional causal logic. The other three–structural, ideational, and psychological may also be at play in a given situation. As an example, there are also indications of ideational causes related to the Muslim faith which influence actions in Somalia. Similarly, ideational causes are present in the ethnic strife among the three communities in BiH. For the purpose of this paper, institutional logic best identifies the path dependence of an action and subsequent unintended consequences. These consequences are keys to understanding stability

30

success or failure. An example is the unintended consequence of donor aid contributing to failing domestic markets in Haiti. Aid affect economic development because the government does not manage donor goods and cannot protect the markets from being overwhelmed. As such, businesses turn away from the markets and economic development stagnates or declines. Where there is no economic development, instability follows.

A study of Somalia and East Timor evaluates externally-imposed systems over the cultivation of indigenous ones. Quickly, a trend is noticed among the two studies directly relating to how individuals and decision makers responsible for state-building regarded and worked with the indigenous population and residual structures. I review state-building actions in Haiti and BiH with respect to the effects of promoting democratic systems over stability. Again, trends readily emerge, making the observation of the unintended consequences easy. How the indigenous people and systems are incorporated still affect the mission, along with the implementation of democracy itself, without consideration of other good governance options.

## Externally Imposed Systems over Indigenous

### Case 1: Somalia

Actors: U.S. Department of State, U.S. Department of Defense, UN Operation in Somalia (I and II), African Union, Non-governmental Organizations

### General History

On the eastern African coast, many world powers sought to conquer Somalia. Arabs brought Islam to the area between the seventh and ten centuries (KMLA 2004) and

Islam remains the dominant religion today. Great powers such as the Chinese, Arabs, Portuguese, Italians, and British, did not leave many permanent settlers as they moved through Somalia. The indigenous tribes or clans remained fairly homogeneous. There are six dominant clan families, four in the north and two in the south. Historically, the northern tribes were pastoral, while the southern clans were agricultural (Acemoglu and Robinson 2012, 238-39).

Political power among the clans is not held by any one person, but is a consensus of the all adult males, or the committees. Clan elders are respected sultans but do not wield unlimited power or influence. Despite violence among the clans, they have a functioning informal government which provides laws for civil conduct, dispute management, land control, and taxation–an enforceable civil code called the *heer*. Sub-families, known as *diya*-paying groups, pay taxes to the larger clan. *Diya* is loosely defined as blood wealth. The clans and *diyas* have always clashed over resources, especially water and grazing rights (Acemoglu and Robinson 2012, 239).

Colonial History

The lands of the ancient Somaale were colonized by the British, French, and Italians during the later part of the 19th century. Each took a portion of the Somali lands. When Somalia gained independence in 1960; its boundaries were formed from British and Italian colonies, and only a portion of the French territory. Interestingly, the British colony did not prosper like most other British colonies, nor were they set up for a more successful transition to independence. Typically, British colonies have fared better after transition than others because of the institutions left behind (Acemoglu and Robinson 2012). Lack of success in British Somalia may in part reflect the northern Somali's nomadic lifestyle. In contrast, the Italian colony was much better established economically (CJA 2011). When the former colonial areas united at independence, observable strengths and weaknesses between them became a source of contention.

FRIDE (*Fundación para las Relaciones Internacionales y el Dialogo Exterior*) comments in a 2005 report that the economic and political conditions in Somalia and other African states are the result of colonialism, the arbitrary border divisions, and imposition of foreign rule (FRIDE 2005, 1). Although foreigners brought elements of the industrial revolution to the Africa states, the political elite did not pro-actively develop their clans beyond immediate needs and existing power relationships (Acemoglu and Robinson 2012, 241). Debates over who is to blame for Somalia's problems are many and pre-date colonization. No foreign power, despite a number of conquerors and years of colonization has been able to fully control Somali tribes. Externally imposed central governments are secondary to the clan system. Without support and acceptance of the clans, an outsider will not have a significant long term affect on the land or population. Clans can be used by the government, but the clans still choose how to wield their power.

## Conflict

The post-colonial government was dislodged from power by a coup in 1969. A military leader, General Siad Barre, took control and leading a socialist type coercive government. Barre's rule created instability, civil strife and exploited clan loyalties (Freedom House 2011). He was ousted in 1991. Since, Somalia has failed to sustain any functioning government, despite years of international assistance. In the meantime, clans fought for control of state resources and criminal enterprises, as a means to sustain their prestige and power. The clan system is strong and power struggle between the clans is undeniable. A fair analogy is "the power of one clan is constrained only by the guns of another" (Acemoglu and Robinson 2012, 80). Civilian deaths during the initial civil war from 1991 to 1992 are estimated at 300,000 people (Freedom House 2011). Deaths were caused not only by tribal fighting, but also because of several years of drought. Without a functioning government, the meager resources held by the state to aid the population were lost to the fighting.

Intervention

Civilian deaths during the 1991-92 conflict prompted a UN- lead humanitarian mission with the U.S. military and various donors in 1992. Objectives of the first UN mission were narrow and focused on the humanitarian issues. Meanwhile, the U.S. military worked to stabilize Mogadishu in order to facilitate the UN mission. The two Somali factions vying for control of the capital were not deterred by the U.S. military presence or the long arm of the UN Security Council. Concerned with the safety of the peace-keepers, the U.S. military was tasked to provide protection for relief efforts for the second UN mission (Dobbins et al. 2003, 55-56).

The military mission, Unified Task Force or UNITAF was sanctioned by UN Security Council Resolution 794, 1992 (Dobbins et al. 2003, 56). It allowed more aggressive military actions to destroy tribal warlords. Attempts for peaceful negotiations did not produce the intended results. Agreements made in January 1993 by clan leaders to facilitate humanitarian aid distribution among other things were unenforceable if compliance faltered. Somalia lacked a governing body to capable of enforcing agreements. Additionally, the clans did not ask for intervention by the UN and U.S. military, so legitimacy of the mission was questionable. The United Nations Operations in Somalia I and its successor, United Nations Operations in Somalia II were not validated by "any legitimate consensual authority from the territorial sovereign. The Somalia mission was not based on the consent of the state, but rather exclusively on Security Council Authority" (Wilde 2007, 36-7).

Primarily, Somalia needed humanitarian relief, but warring factions made that mission near impossible. Despite these problems during the first mission, the UN authorized a second. The second mission would have a broader scope and tried to establish an international territorial administration. Its mission, according to Wilde, was to develop institutions and build capacity (Wilde 2007, 39). UN officers were dispersed as Zone Directors throughout the country to establish rules and procedures for development. However, the directors faced problems with UN malevolence in that they could not access necessary resources for their areas because higher UN leadership did not effectively support the mission beyond the capital (Chopra 2007, 149).

Developing democracy was not necessarily the U.S. military's mission. Since it was part of the second UN mission's mandate, they participated where possible. The UN set about their state-building project which included disarming the warlords militias who were stealing humanitarian aid; securing ports and airfields to facilitate flow of humanitarian aid and develop a democratic government and supporting institutions from local to state levels (Dobbins et al. 2003, 60). Somali population did not have a historical understanding or comprehension of democracy. The first government after independence, a western-style parliamentary system, never took root (Huchthausen 2003, 163). Furthermore, due to Barre's authoritarian regime and its policies through 1991, when the

UN and U.S. military arrived in 1992 and 1993, there were no functioning government systems remaining from which to build upon.

The clans' warlords were the power and they did not want outsiders. In Somalia, foreign powers are not respected among the clans, and therefore, any activity foreigners try to impose is unlikely to be accepted. James Dobbins, John McGinn, Keith Crane, Seth Jones, Rollie Lal, and Andrew Rathmell note that the militias contested the UNs authority to conduct its mission (Dobbins et al. 2003, 60). The simple explanation relates back to Somalia's history and clan fears that increased power by a central government takes power from one or all of the clans. While the U.S. and other international actors going into Somalia had experience with state-building in places like South Korea, Dobbins argues that the experiences were not recent enough (Dobbins 2006, 223) and Somalia was different. The political will of the clans changed quickly and violently; forcing the rapid pull-out of the U.S. military forces.

Unintended Consequences

The UN humanitarian mission was necessary and its intentions good. However, UN and U.S. forces could not overcome the unintended consequences resulting from the path dependency of their actions. Focusing on Parsons institutional causal logic, one can identify three actions which lead to unintended consequences and prevented stability development. The three actions are (1) the imposition of foreign government systems over developing indigenous capability, (2) the Demobilization, Disarmament, and Reintegration program, and (3) humanitarian aid.

Somali political history shows a pattern of rejecting central government propped up or controlled by outsiders. They will question the legitimacy of the outsider and their actions. The UN looked to the UN Security Council resolution to validate legitimacy and authority for their mission, but Wilde notes that Somalia did not consent (Wilde 2007, 37). The U.S. and UN tried to impose central control through a UN transitional government.

The second institutional causal logic relates to the implementation of the Disarmament, Demobilization, and Reintegration plan imposed by the UN. Referencing the quote above regarding clan power, this program would upset the balance of the established power structure among the clans. The program is designed to reduce the number of arms among fighting parties and create opportunities for negotiation. Those who comply receive amnesty from the government for any crimes the individual may have committed against the state. Furthermore, the government has the responsibility to retrain the fighters to be more useful members of society, and aid in bringing other fighters out of hiding. The problem here is that clans will not disarm because it could empower another. There is no entity to enforce program promises, despite the fact that leaders from 15 Somali political groups agreed to disarmament and rehabilitation as part of a four part plan. The support never materialized (Dobbins et al. 2003, 66). This highlights one of the political parties and the clans disconnect; without the clans' support, political promises always fall short or come up empty.

Last, a third institutional causal logic refers to the humanitarian programs. Once again, here is a program that is meant to benefit the whole, but supports the conflict in the end. The weak transitional government was unable to managed distribution so donor agencies relied on local middle-men to distribute the food or resources. However, instead of feeding the masses, the food was diverted to warlords or stolen for recruitment incentives, fighter pay, and feeding individual clan families (Gibson et al. 2005, 89).

The preceding analysis used Parsons's institutional causal logic. There are other causal logics are at play in Somalia. Clans as a whole follow an ideational line. The structure and promulgation of the clan system is prohibitory to central state growth and development. But it is part of their heritage. Somalis identify first with the clan and extended the family second. Power over ones' livelihood is wielded by the clan, not the state. It would be a significant paradigm shift for a Somali to consider his state over his clan. Within the clan there are rules and expectations of conduct among its members. Blood-wealth, or tributes, and feuding are accepted facets of this system; concepts which are unacceptable by liberal, western standards promoted by the U.S. and UN. Imposition of foreign institutions without understanding the informal rules of the land and its people will not achieve the intended objective.

Effects

Centralized government power is not generally recognized by the clans unless it provides some benefit to their survival. Prior to the war, Somalia's government was socialist. The UN mission brought them a democratic system. This system was incongruent with tribal methods of governance and justice. Efforts by foreign powers to control territory outside of the center without consensus of the clans leads to limited and ineffective central government and free reign among clans. Unfortunately, it also limited the UN mission's ability to distribute humanitarian aid throughout the country.

The Disarmament, Demobilization, and Reintegration plan had the unintentional consequence of increasing power among clans. The stronger clans sought greater access

38

to limited state resources that could be sold for more weapons. Such displays of clan strength further emphasized the centralized government's ability to control any aspect of governance. Individuals, who complied with the Disarmament, Demobilization, and Reintegration program, were left with empty promises. The weak transitional government failed to deliver employment or education as part of reintegration. It could not properly coordinate outside support to counter aid discrepancies because the warlords were too strong. Limitations on the part of the government reinforced that personal survival was better if associated to one of the clans over the transitional central government.

Conclusion

The humanitarian missions to Somalia were necessary. When the mission expanded to include the imposition of external systems and democracy, it found no legitimacy in the eyes of Somali warlords. There was no way to separate the two activities, so both suffered. Somalis have accepted outside assistance to settle disputes in the past. They would accept the foreign aid. Once mediation is completed or the crisis averted, foreigners are no longer welcome. The Somalis have their own systems and are capable of functioning in their own way within the clan system. Not all of Somalia is plagued with instability. Somaliland, the northern autonomous region, is the proof. Somaliland has acquired a level of prosperity and stability not matched by any other African state, without international support. The international community does not recognize its declaration of independence from Somalia, but that does not discount Somaliland's accomplishments. According to the failed state index, Somalia has not only consistently ranked with the top ten on the Failed States Index, but has been number one since 2008.

Case 2: East Timor

Actors: UN Mission in East Timor, UN Transitional Administration in East Timor, Timorese, Portugal, Indonesia, Australia

## General History

East Timor is an ancient island northwest of Australia. Today the population is predominantly Catholic, but most still also practice Animism. Religion partly explains domestic attitudes. The island is known for its trade in sandalwood (East Timor Government 2011). Until Portuguese colonists arrived in the 1500s, there was no centralized government among the inhabitants.

## Colonial History

Portugal colonized what is now East Timor in the sixteenth century, however, West Timor, was colonized by the Dutch under their claim to Indonesia. Timorese history claims the colonials neglected their responsibilities to the island and used it as a penal colony. East Timor remained a Portuguese colony in name and only loosely by actions until 1975. Local chiefs along with a Portuguese Governor and Legislative council constituted the governing authorities. Very few Timorese were educated due to lack of investment by the Portuguese (East Timor Government 2011).

In 1974, the new governor legalized political parties. Three parties became dominant, with the *Associação Social Democrática Timorese* (Timorese Social Democratic Association ASDT), later renamed the *Frente Revolucionaria de Timor Leste Independente* or Fretilin being the most dominant. The other two were the *União Democrática Timorense* (Timorese Democratic Union or UDT) and *Associação Popular*

*Democrática Timorese* (Timorese Popular Democratic Association or Apodeti). The latter two parties would collaborate with Indonesian during the occupation. Once the Fretilin took power in 1974, problems quickly emerged between them and the Portuguese. The Fretilin sought independence and demanded support from Portugal to facilitate that end. They also promoted a socialist angle which concerned Indonesia and Australia. Instead of allowing East Timor to become independent under the socialist leaning Fretilin party, Indonesia sought to incorporate East Timor into its territory. A coup by the UDT against the Fretilin in August 1975 made the Portuguese governor. Mário Lemos Pires, flee and he refused to return. Indonesia wanted to take advantage of the situation and tried to make the coup appear as a civil war, but this did not work. Fretilin declared independence in October 1975 and declined integration with Indonesia. The declaration for independence was not recognized. The U.S. supported Indonesia's invasion of East Timor to stop the expansion of communist governments. Indonesia invaded on 7 December 1975 (East Timor Government 2011).

Conflict

Indonesian forces brutally controlled East Timor. They beat, raped, and stole from the Timorese. The Fretilin became a rebel force and harassed Indonesian military forces at every opportunity, while the UDT governed under Indonesian rule. Much like the Fretilin's independence declaration, the UN did not accept the Indonesian regime in East Timor and ordered them to withdraw just days after the invasion (ETAN 2012). Portugal unsuccessfully sought UN intervention to cease the Timorese atrocities at the hands of Indonesian forces. An estimated quarter of the population was killed between 1975 and 1999 (East Timor Government 2011).

International pressure from the UN, allowed East Timor to vote on a referendum for autonomy under Indonesia in 2001. After the Timorese rejected the referendum, but preceding the UN mandate for independence, Indonesian troops razed the entire country, burning and pillaging all villages and towns upon exit (Chopra 2007, 143). East Timor's independence quite literally began on national ruins. The UDT was still partially functioning as a government but had no infrastructure or capital remaining. The UN stepped in to facilitate the transition for statehood by establishing a transitional government.

Intervention

The UN declared East Timor a success when they withdrew their mission in 2005. There was a successful election in 2002, and they were recognized internationally as a state that same year. However, a discussion of East Timor should identify that successes today are attributable of the Timorese not the UN. Even though at the time of intervention the UN had participated in several similar missions, like Somalia and Haiti, those other missions, according to Chopra, actually led to the many poor choices by the UN during mission execution (Robinson 2007, 21).

The UN's state-building efforts had not been all that successful up to this point. An outside observer might think that that lessons learned in other missions were not incorporated, allowing for a repetition of actions whose unintended consequences could be seen as errors. Two actions undertaken by the UN in East Timor created unintended consequences and prevented the emergence of a stable state. These actions are exclusion of political elites in the state-building process and UN officers promoting self interests over Timorese development.

## Unintended Consequences

Given the previous missions undertaken by the UN, Somalia and Haiti for example, actions in East Timor should have been avoided. The UN mission, once the international community finally agreed to support it had good intentions. Ralph Wilde suggests a Trusteeship Council would have been better than the Transitional Administration (Wilde 2007, 42). The UN steered away from Trusteeship because of the colonialism stigma. Chopra called the Transitional Administration choice by the UN to be "state building through UN statehood" (Chopra 2007, 144). The implementation of either a Trusteeship or a Transitional Administration calls into question the legitimacy of the mission itself and the extent of authority employed by the UN over East Timor. Legitimacy does not seem to be as challenging as it was in Somalia, but it supports discussion of the first action of non-inclusion of the political elite.

The non-inclusion of Timorese political elite from decisions related to the transition and positions within the upper levels of the transitional administration, from the institutional causal logic perspective, caused unintended consequences contributing to instability. After the Security Council resolution on East Timor and the Transitional Administration, the UN began institutionalizing external systems in East Timor. This was done without consulting the Timorese political elite. Even though the UDT was still capable of governing, the UN did not strengthen the existing domestic systems. The occupational government was Timorese, primarily of the UDT political party. When planning and execution began, there was no reason to exclude them from the process. On this point, Chopra argues that the UN mission failed because of two key issues. First is the complete absence of the indigenous population as part of the administration or in any aspect of the UN mission. Second, he claims there was "malevolence on the part of the international officials" (Chopra 2007, 144).

The second action, aggrandizement by UN officers, relates back to Chopra's claim of UN officer malevolence. As UN officers took control of their districts or assigned position, they did everything they could to make their section appear better than any other. In doing so, they continued to omit the Timorese to any positions of power or those that would be required upon transition. Lastly, problems among UN offices directly contributed to mission failure. Competition for resources and good reporting to higher compromised support to the Timorese.

Effects

Throughout the entire mission, UN administrators managed every aspect of East Timor, to include a UN civilian police, public services, and agriculture business (Chopra 2007, 150). According to Chopra, the blatant disregard for the Timorese led to a failure by the UN to distinguish power to transition the state and accountability to the population (Chopra 2007, 154).

Disregard for Timorese decisions occurring prior to the UN administration was detrimental for the Timorese and created conflict within the population and hostility toward the UN. For example, before the independence vote, the Timorese government decided to redraw intrastate boundaries, agreeing the consolidated areas would be better and easier for political management. The UN discarded this plan almost immediately, claiming it would be create too much disruption for the domestic population. They did so with an attitude that the Timorese do not know what is good for them so UN officers

44

must make the decisions. Arrogance such as this explains UN officers' disregard for the Timorese people as a whole.

The corollary competition among regions for resources prohibited or hindered domestic development, to include vital infrastructure projects. The UN controlled rebuilding plans, but internal problems prevented local administrators to adequately access funds for construction at lower districts. Officer aggrandizement and personal promotion focuses ensured most development never expanded beyond the capital. The transitional administration employed a flawed system that failed to develop the population and prepare them for full governance as an independent state.

Conclusion

The UN reinforced plans within the externally imposed system that contrasted the desires of the Timorese. The results of these actions increased tension in among the Timorese, obstructed coordination among UN district officers responsible for development, created instability, and failed to produce the lasting institutional development promised by the UN. Repeatedly, the UN officers and policies disregarded Timorese needs and their voice. East Timor had a functioning government leading into independence but needed help in the transition. The Fretilin continued to contest the UDT government as incapable of good governance under Indonesian oversight. Given the physical conditions of the state after the extraction of Indonesian troops, East Timor desperately needed outside help to rebuild existing institutions, not supplant them with the ideal UN state. When the UN withdrew, East Timor was not in a better political or economic situation. UN actions left the Timorese feeling betrayed by the UN. Since 2002 the annual failed state index has ranked East Timor in the top 20. The Freedom House

45

index categorizes the state as partly free, indicating that there is not a full democracy functioning and instability remains.

## Discussion of Externally Imposed Systems over Indigenous

Is there any condition where the foreign institution imposition is good? There are several examples where such impositions, with minor modifications, have succeeded and aided in the development of the state. A colonial history or even periods of civil war do not prevent colonies from becoming successful. States such as the Dominican Republic and New Zealand successfully made the transition from colony to statehood like India. The concerns of this paper are not of colonial heritage, but the actions of external imposition of systems in modern times and how it contributes to instability.

The first action is lack of connection and coordination with the local population. When the local population is dismissed or otherwise not allowed active participation in development, they will by and large, not have ownership of the system. Repeatedly, in the case studies the intervening actors installed a system that is comfortable and manageable for them, typically westerners, but may or may not match the needs of the population.

The disregard for local institutions, capability, and resilience of population is the second action. Too often the intervener finds domestic institutions to be substandard knowing what they (the intervener) can bring to the situation. This could also be considered arrogant on the part of the intervener. Fukuyama notes that in Haiti, Somalia, East Timor, and Bosnia, "the international community in various guises stepped into each of these conflicts–often too late and with too few resources–and in several cases ended up literally taking over the governance functions from local actors" (Fukuyama 2006, 93).

Additionally, Fukuyama warns that imposition of outside services prevent successful transfer of authority back to the local population because they do not have the skills or foreign resources to sustain them (Fukuyama 2006, 241-242).

## Democratization over Stability

### Case 1: Haiti

Actors: U.S. Department of Defense, U.S. Department of State, UN Mission in Haiti (1994), UN Humanitarian Commission on Human Rights, International Monetary Fund, UN Stability Mission in Haiti (2004), Organization of American States, Non-governmental Organizations, President Jean –Bertrand Aristide, Haiti political elite, Lavalas Party

### General History

An island nation in the Caribbean, Haiti has been inhabited for thousands of years. The largest pre-colonial population was the Taínos (Haitian Pearl 2012). Taíno chiefdoms dotted the Caribbean islands and they were enemies with other Caribbean tribes. Chiefs provided rule of law and could be male or female. Society in general had two classes, commoners and nobles. Healers and priests held a special place in society. Like so many other native populations, the Taínos were all but destroyed by foreign diseases carried by the colonists. Taíno culture significantly affected Haitian society even as it transitioned into a slave state.

### Colonial History

Columbus landed on Haiti in 1492 and named the land Hispaniola. Spain colonized the area later. The Spanish were brutal in their control of the land, going so far as to cut off the natives' hands if they failed to pay taxes or tribute as deemed necessary by the Spanish representative. As more colonists arrived, natives succumbed to the diseases brought by the colonists. In the early 1500s the natives unsuccessfully revolted against the Spanish. Due to the revolt and decrease number of natives available to work, Spain began importing Africans who they employed as slave labor (Haitian Pearl 2012).

Hispaniola was geographically important for the movement of goods and military forces within the Caribbean. By the 1600s, settlers also now referred to the island as Santo Domingo. Natural resources were not present in significant quantities to exploit, but the island remained strategically important for colonial powers seeking control in the new world. In the late seventeenth century, France assumed control over the western part of Hispaniola, now modern day Haiti. They renamed the area Saint-Domingue (Haitian Pearl 2012). More African slaves were brought to the island, forever changing the demographics. Both the Catholic religion and voodoo were common among slave labor. By the late nineteenth century, there were three main populations: the colonists, free blacks and mixed race people, and the slaves. Each group distrusted the others. Non-whites often accused colonists of abuse. This was not a homogeneous environment.

A former slave and military leader, Toussaint l'Ouverture, worked with France to gain control of the territory in 1801 after another slave revolt. He led a dictatorial rule but quickly removed by Napoleon Bonaparte. This power shift did not last long as two of l'Ouverture's close military leaders orchestrated and led the revolt which ultimately drove out the French. Former Haitian slaves became the new political elite; once in control, they gained independence in 1804 (Girard 2010, 156-157).

Conflict to remove the French severely affected the already weak agricultural infrastructure because of recent natural disasters. Due to geography, the island was and remains susceptible to natural disasters such as hurricanes and earthquakes. Governance compounded with problems from natural disasters, led Jean-Jacques Dessalines, L'Ouverture's former general, to decide that a firm hand was the only way to rule if he meant to build the nation and make it viable. His tenure was marked by military dominance. At independence, the Haitian people did not have the knowledge or resources to be a successful state. The French legacy was to leave Haitians uneducated and unskilled. The infrastructure was designed to support French requirements and until 1801, had no Haitians at any level of meaningful governance (Haitian Pearl 2012).

Military strong men rose and fell so quickly that Dessalines' vision for Haitian development never materialized. Increased Haitian violence and fears that the island could be used strategically against allied forces during the First World War forced U.S. intervention in 1915, which was the first attempt to democratize Haiti. During their 19-year tenure, the U.S. altered the face of Haiti, at least physically, if not socially. They employed the local population to build schools, roads, and other infrastructure, but did not address the root causes of instability (Haitian Pearl 2012).

Conflict

A state in nearly constant turmoil, I now focus on what brought the U.S. back to Haiti in 1994. Brutality of the colonial experience, according to Philippe Girard, paved the way for tensions within the populations and poor governance in general (Girard 2010, 155). The political elite that accompanied each strong man leader continued to practice extractive measures, much like the colonial rulers before them. They did so both before

49

and after U.S. intervention. The democratic system established by the U.S. did not take root. By 1960 when François Duvalier, or Papa Doc, took control of Haiti it was anything but a democracy. Papa Doc's policies and those of his son, Bébé Doc kept development and industrialization at bay. The Duvalier's were more interested in retaining power than developing the country (Girard 2010, 158).

Bébé Doc went into exile in 1986 after a popular uprising and calls to step down by the U.S. (BBC 2012). Power struggles ensued until the country held hold elections in 1990 (Girard 2010, 161). Jean-Bertrand Aristide, a former priest, was elected president. This democratic victory collapsed months later when the military overthrew Aristide (Somit and Peterson 2005, 43). Despite being an elected representative, Aristide's policies and practices differed little from that of the Duvaliers. He did implement some positive reforms, but also continued extractive practices to enrich himself and his supporters.

Intervention

Operation Restore Democracy deployed U.S. military forces to Haiti in 1994. The UN initiated a mission that same year. Per their mission, the U.S. sought to restore the elected president to power. In doing so, they neglected other aspects of development that could have improved security and brought relief to the population. Meanwhile, the population who suffered under poor governance for generations was in dire need of humanitarian aid. Donors and international agencies responded in droves to meet that need. The government had no means to monitor or control the substantial donations.

The UN considered the Haitian mission a success after Aristide returned to power. However, long term results were not as impressive. Pei, Samia Amin, and Seth Garz note that Haiti was a failed state less than ten years later. They blame the U.S. and UN's ability to "balance local legitimacy with the retention of coercive authority" (Pei et al. 2006, 69) for long term stability. Similarly, Dobbins claims the UN abandoned the mission "before lasting improvement in Haiti's chronic misgovernance could be effected" (Dobbins 2006, 220). Whose responsibility was it to look beyond the reinstallation of an elected official as opposed to assessing the situation for a valid solution to conflict?

Unintended Consequences

Parsons's institutional causal logic identifies three actions for consideration of their unintended consequences. The three actions are: reinforcement of an elected official who rules non-democratically; lack of investment in domestic capability; and donor support preventing economic development. A problem with democracy imposition over stability in Haiti is that the U.S. and UN supported democracy in name, but not in deed.

The first action is the support of a democratically elected official who rules as an autocrat. Aristide's rule was not democratic. Freedom House reports going back to 2002 continually list Haiti as partially free. This indicates that it does not meet western democratic standards. Aristide neglected domestic institutions and capabilities by employing extractive economics and policies. Although Aristide left office peacefully in 1996, the new president was his hand-picked successor who allowed Aristide to retain a prominent role in the government. He was re-elected in the 2000 elections, only to be ousted again in 2004 (Pearson and Lounsbery 2012, 70; Somit and Peterson 2005, 43). A recent example of this same behavior is that of Vladimir Putin in Russia.

The second action is the lack of investment, both economically and politically, in Haiti by the U.S. and UN. During the first Haiti mission, the emphasis was restoring

51

Aristide to power. Very little effort was given to improve domestic systems, institutions, or infrastructure. Pei et al. and Dobbins consider this an oversight in the UN mission and one of the reasons Haiti failed (Pei et al. 2006, 69; Dobbins 2006, 220). When the U.S. and UN went back to Haiti in 2004, the conditions were worse than they had been ten years earlier. Only the political elite supporting Aristide were free from suffering the effects of drought and repeated natural disasters. Once again, the mission was to return Aristide to power. Domestic development was a lower priority. The second mission did not improve democracy or domestic institutions.

Donor support is the third action which led to instability in Haiti. The government did little to support the state's economic development, despite years of receiving international aid. Haiti does not have abundant natural resources. It depends on commercial industries and aid to maintain its economy. Haiti receives money from the International Monetary Fund. As of 2011, it had done so for over 35 years (Nelson and Wallace 2012, 112n18). Girard notes that the common theory why Haiti is so poor is because of its over dependence on neighbors (Girard 2010, 155).

Effects

Even though Aristide returned to power, democracy remained in the shadows. Haitians remained uneducated on the citizen and political responsibilities within a democracy. They continued to operate by rules and regulations they understand which are not necessarily democratic, such as black markets as a means to obtain goods the government should provide but do not. Given this tendency, one could argue that the U.S. and UN should have done more to develop domestic systems which the population recognizes and give them legitimacy. Overlooking this aspect of society and its capabilities and only passively supporting democracy by reinstating the elected strong man, taught Haitians nothing about democracy. Increasingly, they grow despondent to the promises of democracy, when nothing changes that affects their daily lives.

According to Somit and Peterson, when the missions ended Haiti was left with insufficient security forces, weak political systems, a poverty stricken populations, no investment in the economic system and no measures to curb corruption among the military and political elite (Somit and Peterson 2005, 43-44). Dobbins et al. concur and add the absence of rule of law or sufficient justice system (Dobbins et al. 2003, 72-73). Without a strong basic economic system, it is extremely difficult to advance good governance, let alone the challenges of a democracy. Fareed Zakaria notes that democracy can only be sustained in an environment with stable political and economic systems (Zakaria 2003). The effects of the third action also complicate the economic action.

Domestic markets were failing because of donor contributions. Because the government did not monitor and manage donations, it cannot prevent markets from being overwhelmed with goods, thereby contributing to the destruction of the domestic economy. Examples of this are seen in Haitian agriculture and textile markets. Agricultural growth, specifically the market for grains and rice is unproductive or stagnant due to large donations of grains from the U.S. Domestic subsidies are not sufficient to allow Haitian farmers sell their product at a fair price because of foreign aid and supplements overwhelm the market (Girard 2010, 160). Textiles are also affected. Clothes shipped from the U.S. and other states prevent domestic growth. The overabundance of clothes such as t-shirts and jeans has all but destroyed the textile market because it cannot compete against donations. Repeatedly, domestic markets are impeded and absent of growth or development because of foreign aid, keeping Haiti in a cycle of poverty. Weak government systems prevent Haiti from properly managing the influx of donor monies and goods (Pei et al. 2006, 73).

Conclusion

Haiti's history with strong man governance demonstrates how Haitians and their political leaders relate to democracy. Issues, partly institutional and partly ideational, continue to afflict Haiti with instability and poverty. The Dominican Republic continues to improve its economic and political standings. The U.S. and UN focus on restoring democracy in Haiti, which in the end only reinstated the elected strong-man. It did not employ significant resources to develop domestic institutions or prevent further neglect at the hands of the President and his supporters. Additional the extractive practices of the governing elite, high illiteracy rates, and what Paine calls "leadership deficit" (Paine 2010, 307) are as damaging. Frederic Pearson and Marie Lounsbery, and others, posit that they only way to keep Haiti on the democratic path is with continued foreign intervention (Pearson and Lounsbery 2012, 71; Peksen 2012, 81).

Case 2: Bosnia and Herzegovina

Actors: U.S. Department of Defense, U.S. Department of State, North Atlantic Treaty organization, Council of the European Union, non-governmental organizations, UN Office of the High Representative

## General History

BiH was conquered repeatedly over the centuries by Roman, Ottomans, and others. Slavic in origin, is has been home to multiple ethnicities at any given time. There are three significant ethnic populations: Bosnians or Bosniacs (predominantly Muslim), Bosnian Serbs (predominantly Orthodox Christian), and Bosnian Croats (predominantly Roman Catholic).

Islam arrived in the late fourteenth and early fifteenth centuries with the Ottoman Empire. A degree of religious leniency within the Ottoman Empire allowed Orthodox Christianity to continue under their rule. All BiH citizens speak Serbo-Croatian, a Slavic language. There is a difference among the groups regarding the written word. Croats and Bosnian Muslims use a Latin based script and the Serbs use the Cyrillic alphabet (Sells 1996, 5).

## Colonial History

Bosnia had a unique experience with colonial powers. They were not governed by western powers such as Britain or France. They were, however, incorporated into Yugoslavia after the First World War, which was suspended during the Second World War. Marshall Josip Broz Tito reconstituted the Federation of Yugoslavia in 1945 (Sells 1996, 5). He maintained a delicate balance among the multi-ethnic Yugoslavia during the Cold War. According to Sells, by the 1970s Tito had "found a strategic niche between Soviet and Western spheres." The three dominant ethnic groups in Bosnia–Serbs, Croats, and Bosniacs, had their nationalist fervencies kept in check by Tito's strong arm tactics under communist rule. When Tito died in 1980, successors were able to maintain Tito's "brotherhood and unity" ideal long enough for Yugoslavia to host the 1984 Winter

Olympics in Sarajevo (Sells 1996, 7). This unity began to fall apart by 1987 and further deteriorated after the precipitous decline of the Union of Soviet Socialist Republics beginning in 1989 with the fall of the Berlin Wall.

Conflict

When the former Socialist Republic of Yugoslavia collapsed in 1991, BiH emerged as a socialist state. This is not surprising given the politics of the former Yugoslavia. Serbia was the strongest of the Yugoslavian states and had dominant Serbian populations in the other states. Typically, the Serbs held the majority in government. Specific to Bosnia, Serbs became very aggressive and political entities began fighting over independence. Although succession from the failed Yugoslavia was accepted in 1992, ethnic tensions boiled over and lead to atrocities by all three groups against the others. Some of these instances can be found in Michael Sells' 1996 book, *The Bridge Betrayed: Religion and Genocide in Bosnia*.

Significant international intervention came after the 1995 Srebrenica massacre. In July 1995, Serbian military killed hundreds of Muslim men in Srebrenica even though it was a declared UN safe area for Muslim refugees fleeing from Serbian annihilation. The UN organized a mission in Bosnia and sent a small contingent of forces to aid the refugees. General Ratko Mladic was the Serbian military leader ordering the massacre among other atrocities during the war. As of May 2012, he is awaiting trial at The Hague for his actions in Srebrenica and in Bosnia in general. Notably, he mocked the Dutch commander of the UN forces for his inability to stop Serbian troops from killing (Sells 1996, 27).

## Intervention

The U.S., NATO and the UN intervened in BiH in 1995 to quell violence and stop ethnic cleansing among its citizens. Intervention and subsequent missions were meant to create a stable state, bring harmony among the three ethnic populations, and produce a sovereign democracy. More than fifteen years of international missions has left Bosnia more fragmented than before the war. Actions by the UN and its Office of the High Representative in particular have not facilitated a harmonious relationship among the three groups, and stability is tenuous in the absence of control by the international community.

When international forces first entered Bosnia, their mission was to prevent more atrocities through peace-enforcement. From there, it quickly shifted to establishing a democratic government. The vehicle to meet these objectives was the Dayton Peace Accord, brokered by U.S. President Clinton. The Dayton Peace Accord is a source of great discontent. The actions discussed here and their unintended consequences relate back to the Dayton Peace Accord. The three actions addressed with the institutional causal logic in this case study are elections (timing and process), forced integration of political parties at state level but allowance for two presidential-led republics and the Brčko district, and UN officers power management.

## Unintended Consequences

Parsons' institutional causal logic is used to evaluate key actions in this state-building activity where democracy promotion over stability failed to produce the intended results. Furthermore, it will help to identify the unintended consequences associated with those actions. Events for evaluation include the election process and the political and ethnic division of BiH. Both of these events stem from the imposition of the 1995 Dayton Peace Accord.

Elections are considered the primary tool that allows a state to declare democracy. However, elections can be problematic and do not guarantee democratic rights within a state. Even though international actors such as the UN and their monitoring agency, the Organization for Security and Cooperation in Europe, are aware of this conundrum, they continue to promote elections in unstable communities under the belief that elections will create unity among the disjointed citizens. Elections are the first action considered in this analysis using institutional causal logic.

Just one year after the conflict ended, the UN, enforcing the Dayton Peace Accord, helped Bosnia hold its first round of elections. UN observers declared the elections free and fair despite disruption at some polling stations. Military peace-keepers were influential in deterring significant violence. Elected officials in the two republics were selected from the population majority by running on nationalist platforms. Some watch groups, such as the International Crisis Group, denigrate the UN mission for pushing elections so soon after conflict (ICG 1996). They claim it allowed political leaders to solidify around obstructive (to state development) platforms (Talentino 2004, 566).

The second action addresses the political structure and is directly related to elections. Specifically in how the political structure under the Dayton Peace Accord intended to integrate ethnicities at the state level, yet it inherently allowed for ethnic division due to the separate republics. Institutional causal logic identifies that this political formula increases tensions between ethnicities rather than unify them under one state. To begin, the Dayton Peace Accord established the presidency as a shared responsibility among the three ethnicities; the elected rotate every eight months. However, the supreme executive power in the state is not the president; it is the senior Office of the High Representative officer (European Forum 2012). There are two republics, the Federation of BiH and the *Republica Srpska*. Serbs are now the majority in the *Republica Srpska*, while Bosniacs and Croats are the majority in the Federation.

Effects

The unintended consequences of democratization over stability development in Bosnia are still unfolding because the effects of these actions were long reaching. On the issue of elections, a 2010 FRIDE report on democracy from the recipients' point of view notes that in BiH, there is a "disconnect between the project and political level of external actors' strategies" (FRIDE 2010, 10). This suggests that the project of democratization is in contrast with how politics are played in the republics and at the state level. The political end state desired by the Office of the High Representative cannot be accomplished, because of the constraints within the Dayton Peace Accord. Elections in Bosnia have done little to quell hostilities or develop trust among divided parties.

The Dayton Peace Accord created a very complicated democratic government system and elections should have given the indigenous population a sense of control by selecting their political leaders. The FRIDE Democracy Backgrounder from September 2008 claims the complicated system actually made the indigenous population less interested in actively participating in elections (FRIDE 2008, 2). This is debatable. But what is clear is that elected officials continue to rally around nationalist platforms. Problems remain at local levels in areas of political and judicial corruption. Furthermore,

59

members of the minority population are not expected to win any office within the republics, because of continued nationalist (ethnic) rhetoric.

Moving to the problem of the divided republic, the effects obviously created political divisions which reinforced ethnic tensions. Outlined in the Dayton Peace Accord, the UN intentionally allowed the separate republics to operate as 'Bosnia.' One problem with the separate republics is that the situation resembles a partitioning, similar to that of Pakistan and India. Early Serb action calls sought a very similar outcome (Sells 1996, 15-16).

The republics have a culture all of their own, based on the majority population. As a result, minorities in either republic still complain of policy or political abuse and negligence by the majority against them. Political rhetoric from the *Republica Srpska* is overly nationalist (ethnic), reminiscent of the emboldened statements made by Serbs prior to the outbreak of war in 1992. The exercise of bringing unity through divisive republics under one democracy has not created a path for stability.

## Conclusion

Scholars such as Talentino and Chandler and international think tanks like FRIDE agree that stability in BiH is not a sure thing after the remaining UN officers and agencies depart. Elections continue to be a problem. At the state level, the October 2010 elections failed to bring parties to the table to form a state government for fifteen months. The UN still has administrative control at the state level and can override decisions by the tri-presidents office under Bonn Powers from the Dayton Peace Accord. Since the elected presidents have limited powers until the Office of the High Representative departs, one might suggest that the population does not recognize them as anything more than

60

figureheads. In 2007, Chandler states that the "Bosnian state still lacks a secure basis in Bosnian society and commands little social or political legitimacy" (Chandler 2007, 85). Given the problems after the 2010 elections to form the government, Chandler's assessment continues to have merit. Non-acceptance by the population creates other unintended consequences such as loss of faith or perceptions of illegitimacy of the government.

Democracy in each of the republics is a democracy only in that there are elections, but corruption and rule of law violations prevent real democratic advances. Challenges to unify all of Bosnia under one democracy and curb ethnic tensions relate directly to the conditions established by and limitations of the Dayton Peace Accord. This discussion causes one to ask, could stability have been established if the former political system had been reconstituted instead of deploying democratic systems? There does not seem to be sufficient analysis on the value of reconstitution over the flat implementation of democracy. Meanwhile, stability and security suffer as crime, corruption, and ethnic divisions increase.

## Discussion of Democratization over Stability

The cases of Haiti and BiH demonstrate actions and unintended consequences of democratization over stability. Emphasizing democracy before stability does not necessarily lead to the long-term stability goal of state-building. Three main challenges or observations resonating from the discussion are: inclusion of the indigenous population at all levels, education of political elite and citizens, and growth and development retardation due to donor aid.

The first challenge to achieving long-term stability lies with non-inclusion of the population, which was also present in the discussion of foreign imposition. Failure to incorporate the domestic population in the development process negatively affects long-term stability from state-building. Incorporation was better in Bosnia than in Haiti. However, the over watch and influence of UN officers partially negates the inclusion because Bosnia did not own the process. Repeatedly, the domestic population expresses one thing, but international actors charge ahead with their singularly focused democratization plan. Despite the civil break-down in Bosnia, there were former political leaders may have been able to facilitate stability and cohesion.

Even when the government ceases to function, there remains a shadow infrastructure that supports the population. This system may not be perfect, but might be a starting point for developing indigenous systems and looking for leaders to be a part of the state-building endeavor. Incorporating elements of shadow infrastructures may produce a system more acceptable with the domestic population as opposed to forcing a foreign system on them amid chaos. The Dayton Peace Accord is a source of many problems in establishing and maintaining democracy in Bosnia. Allowing for the two distinct republics within the state divides the people and reinforces nationalistic (ethnic) attitudes. This creates problems of its own, discussed elsewhere. But in terms of population inclusion or non-inclusion, the UN considered it an action of inclusion. Hence, the action becomes an example of good intentions producing poor outcomes. According to the commentary above, this concession of multiple republics and the special area of Brcko actually reinforced national (ethnic) and religious divisions.

Haiti also had a functioning government under military leadership before the return of Aristide. One could argue that an opportunity was missed by emphasizing Aristide's reinstatement over identifying and addressing the reasons he was ousted; finding the root cause of the situation. Haiti still had no understanding of democracy; especially since Aristide's attitudes and behavior were similar to past, non-democratic leaders. The inclusion problem in Haiti is that state-builders failed to incorporate the voices of the opposition leaders and the population in general.

In order to include the population, education is fundamental. The second observation regarding emphasis of democracy over indigenous development is democratic education. If a democracy is to be successful it must be understood by the population. Without education, the population has little value for civic duty, government responsibilities, or rule of law. This triune reflects the checks and balance system expected within a democracy. Elections are only one part of the broader democratic experience.

Democratic education in Haiti or Bosnia did not exist. It is possible that the UN could establish an office dedicated to democratic education. Even if the political elite fully understood democracy, especially in Haiti, there are indications they actively sought to curtail democracy and associated development for fear of losing personal and positional power. Therefore, the state did not properly educate the population of their civic duties and expectations of government service, as the political elite did not want them to exercise it (Pei et al. 2006, 72). Somit and Peterson state that, "Haiti is a classic illustration, then, of the difficulty encountered by a major power trying to impose democratic structures on a country with a long-tradition of strong man-rule, military dictatorship, and the like, without being willing to invest time, resources, and personnel" (Somit and Peterson 2005, 44). Bosnia's problem with democracy is different because ethnic tensions overshadow it. Additionally, there is the level of power the Office of the High Representative still holds in contrast to that of the elected government. If international actors do not supply resources to train and educate the population and political elite on democracy, instability is likely because elections alone are insufficient to transform a political system.

Haiti and Bosnia have received donor assistance for decades. The third observation is the influence of donor capital and resources. Even good intention donor capital can cause unintended consequences, as highlighted in Haiti. When state-building missions focus on democracy over stability, the resulting system is weak but dependent upon an influx of donor capital and resources. Donor aid is expected and welcome, but too often the government is too weak to manage the influx; or a plan is not implemented and followed that incorporates the aid when needed, then moves toward self-sustainment. If democracy cannot stand alone, in short order, donor support can actually hamper development and create dependency cycles. It can also create opportunities for existing corruption and patronage systems among those with access to the donor aid to further exploit good intentions for their own purposes. In some instances, it can even prevent the intended recipient from receiving the aid, because of malfeasance by political elite.

State-building missions are resource intensive. Interveners want a plan while their constituents want to know that money was well spent and that lost lives, if any, were for a good cause. To withdraw with dignity, it is in their best interests to ensure what has been developed can be maintained beyond donor exit. "It is precisely the creation of self-

sustaining local institutions that provides a graceful exit strategy for the outsiders"
(Fukuyama 2006, 242). Moreover, if the intervener does not want to go back in, they
need to ensure the state is more than just functional; it is capable.

## Summary of Findings and State-Building Theory

### Findings

State-building is a difficult task. It is also resource intensive. In order for stability
to emerge through state-building one might reconsider a heavy emphasis on
democratization or dependency on external systems over indigenous methods and
governance. The case studies reveal three actions routinely committed by intervening
powers such as the UN or the U.S. during state-building activities. Referencing Ernest
Gellner's essay, "Nations and Nationalism" related to spread of African independence,
Sutton remarks that during colonization (read any form of government that operates
similarly) despite lacking common backgrounds within a colony, the people were "held
together by the administration and control of a colonial government that imposed a
language, laws and regulations, so that there came to be a social identity distinctive to
that territory" (Sutton 2006, 44). There are other historical examples of where such
patterns produced stable states, for a period, such as Yugoslavia. The state provided a
unifying symbol or action to galvanize the population. Where the population is
heterogeneous it makes sense to find elements from within the narrative of the people to
build consensus.

Once a colony becomes independent, it was not necessarily prepared for self-
sufficiency. Haiti was not prepared for independence. The colonial French were notorious
for not incorporating indigenous populations at high levels within the governing

structure. Therefore, in 1804, despite gaining independence, leader motivation for self-rule was insufficient as they lacked sufficient governance knowledge. The default was to mimic or replicate colonial management styles using the extractive institutions of colonial legacy, patronage, and other tendencies which created divisions between the elite and general population. Similarly, in Bosnia, Tito controlled the population but only suppressed ethnic rivalries. As a result, the loss of Tito's strong rule allowed suppressed rivalries to rise. One argument in this paper is that the domestic population is important. The rise and fall of the former Yugoslavia is a recent example of just how quickly stability can degrade when political elite focus more on a system than in the development of the population and state as a whole.

## State-Building Theory

Reviewing analysis from the four case studies (Somalia, East Timor, Haiti, and BiH) the following theory emerges: if U.S. or other western state policy makers want to foster stability in other countries via state-building, they should prioritize the cultivation of indigenous systems (economic, security, judicial, and social) over externally-imposed systems and stability over democratization. Before advancing into the case studies and theory development, the literature led me to make two assumptions. The first is that the world leaders are so overly committed to democratic promotion that they become blind to other opportunities to establish stable, secure environments. The second is that domestic population will reject foreign systems that conflict with their historical values and societal patterns. A caveat to the second is that this repudiation can be mitigated with education and inclusion. When challenging the theory or considering future research, it is necessary to keep this perspective in mind.

66

To test the theory, more rigorous study should explore the two main issues and two themes presented in my findings. The two main issues are to incorporate the domestic population at all levels of development and to nurture existing domestic activities, structures, and institutions. My themes are to minimize the effects donor or foreign aid dependency and understand that each country's problems (leading to intervention) were the result of internal rather than external conditions. Case study observations warn against combining state-building and democratic promotion endeavors if these issues are ignored. The issues and themes are interrelated and directly encourage the integration of the domestic populace, and its structures and institutions. Integration of domestic systems may include those that are contrary to western ideals but may be the bridge needed to build self-sustaining systems that meet domestic needs and understanding in order to prevent a pariah state.

Involvement or incorporation of the local population into the development process is the first area of discussion. If we take heed of Ghani and Lockhart, where "the first task in moving a country from conflict to stability is to formulate rules to ensure that stakeholders acknowledge each other's claims within a framework of politics rather than violence" (Ghani and Lockhart 2009, 180). This actually refers to bringing all parties to the table for peace talks, but is equally applicable for interveners to consider before embarking on state-building and democratization without consent of the population. Consider the previous discussion on domestic populations accepting international state-building missions as legitimate. Talentino suggests that overlooking the population in terms of nation-building will lead to problems with state-building at the domestic level

(Talentino 2004, 563). Population is a key consideration and can complicate short-range goals.

Second is disregard for domestic activities, structures and institutions. Related to this is the arrogance of individuals going into a mission that precludes a dialogue in the value of domestic activities, structures, or shadow institutions. Chopra reflects on the resilience of the population despite international activity, stating "the fact that the population continued to exist, that market forces of whatever kind are always at work, and that the social structures of indigenous communities invariably generate sources of political legitimacy according to their own paradigm" (Chopra 2007, 142). Regardless of what system is emplaced, the domestic population will circumvent the intended process unless or until it conforms to their norms and expectations or is a reflection of their values.

The first theme relates to dependency upon donor aid. In efforts to promote democratization, donors push monies and resources onto the state. While the intent is good, the side effects are often less than desirable. In Haiti, donations of clothing all but destroyed the textile industry. Domestic agriculture also suffered under the receipt of U.S. surplus (Girard 2010, 160). Cycles of dependency emerged in East Timor, Haiti, and Somalia. All of which stifles domestic political and economical growth. Donor aid is expected and welcome, but must be managed so that it reaches the intended recipients and does not negate domestic markets.

My second theme addresses the fact that each country's problems (leading to intervention) were the result of internal rather than external conditions. Interveners should help find solutions to the core problems for why intervention occurred in the first place. This is not an easy task. Without addressing grievances the issue will resurface, as evidenced in the four case studies. The key to successful state-building is as much on the international actors providing guidance and resources as it is dependent on the recipient state.

# CHAPTER 5

## CONCLUSIONS AND RECOMMENDATIONS

### Conclusions

This paper analyzed four case studies (Somalia, East Timor, Haiti, and BiH) and drew observations to create a state-building theory. Case studies spanned an eleven-year period from 1991 to 2002. Foreign intervention continues in all of these states, reinforcing the idea that they are not stable states. I theorize that the cultivation of indigenous systems (economic, security, judicial, and social) over externally-imposed systems and focusing on stability over democratization will give decision makers the tools necessary to foster stability in other countries via state-building. Furthermore, case study analysis suggests successful state-building must incorporate the domestic population at all levels of development and nurture existing domestic activities, structures, and institutions. They must also effectively minimize negative effects of donor or foreign aid dependency and address internal strife within the recipient state. Literature identifies these two issues and two themes as part of the broader discussions of state-building and security matters; but they are largely ignored or partially explored during actual state-building missions.

State-building will continue so long as there are weak, failing, and failed states. Typically, but not exclusively conducted by the UN, state-building has become routine for the world powers like the U.S. However, there is nothing necessarily routine about the why and when foreign powers initiate state-building. Problem sets are unique to each state. Similarities may exist, but it is misleading to create a plan of action significantly from a previous endeavor. The same can be said about the imposition of democratic institutions as part of state-building activities.

Democracy may not be right for all weak, failed, and failing states; nor does the indigenous population necessarily want it. There is a level of economic development along with democratic education and instruction that should occur before democratic system imposition. The emphasis should be on building stable structures. Paris notes that "the very strategy that peace builders have employed to consolidate peace–political and economic liberalizations–seems paradoxically, to have increased the likelihood of renewed violence in several of these states" (Paris 2004, 6). Given this study, one could reason that Paris' observation stands because of the UN and other actors' such as the U.S's misalignment of priorities during the state-building effort.

Security is the concern of all states. Most western nations reference the possible threat of weak, failing, and failed states in national security reviews and White Papers. Ungoverned spaces can present an international threat, the Somali pirates are a good example. Yet, ineffective state-building operations are just as dangerous to long-term peace and stability.

Recommendations

Hypotheses to consider

To stand on alone, theories should be testable. Parsons's institutional causal logic facilitated findings of two main issues and identified two correlating themes. The short duration of the case studies presents an opportunity for further research. It would be informative to expand the number of cases as well as the overall time period to evaluate if the same issues or themes emerge. An expanded study may identify that world powers are learning from past endeavors and employing more successful strategies. Each theory component is subject to testing as are the observations. The theory suggests that adhering to plans which incorporate these components in development will increase stable states as a strategic end to state-building activity. It is understood that the activities challenged in this paper do not occur in isolation, nor are they interdependent. Therefore, the findings are subject to criticism and dispute.

Regarding follow-on research, two hypotheses might be considered that if examined prior to initiating a state-building program, could positively affect state-building efforts leading to stable states.

H1: State-building activity occurring separate from democratization development will produce more long term gains in security.

H2: Incorporation of domestic population, structures, and functioning institutions into development plan lead to greater participation and acceptance among the local populace, which equates to more durable systems.

State-building activities have become a program of democratization to the detriment of developing states. Reasons for intervention vary from state to state. It is imperative to assess each situation independently. Doing so allows the intervener to properly identify functioning institutions, evaluate the reasons for state weakness or failure, and develop plans appropriate to the goals of the weak state. An end state of liberal democracy from state-building by intervening states such as the U.S. might be valid in some situations, but not all. State-building has to incorporate the goals of the recipient state, too. Achieving stability creates a permissive environment for economic and political development appropriate for the state in question.

In sum, I argue that policymakers should prioritize the cultivation of indigenous structures and stability by attending to indigenous officials, populations, and systems from the local to national levels. This theory has implications for policymakers considering state-building efforts as a way to increase their respective state's security.

# GLOSSARY

Extractive economic institutions: Designed by political elite to enrich themselves and perpetuate power at the expense of the population and state development (Acemoglu and Robinson 2012, 399).

Extractive institutions: Prevent economic growth, resist democratization, perpetuates patrimonialism, and widens the gap between rich and poor.

Extractive political institutions: Concentrate power in the hands of a narrow elite an place few constraints on the exercise of this power (Acemoglu and Robinson 2012, 81).

Ideational Causal Mechanism: Related to culture, values, beliefs, and or communal attributes (Parsons 2007, 12).

Institutional Causal Mechanism: Refers to formal and informal rules and organizations, and path dependency leading to unintended consequences is the key identifier (Parsons 2007, 12).

International Administration: Full responsibility for the functions of the government, in reference to the UN application of International Territorial Administrations.

Nation-building: The development and merger of the people and cultures within a define boundary.

Psychological Causal Mechanism: A perspective that is common to all man, commonly associated with Prospect Theory and Relative Deprivation Theory explaining irrational outcomes (Parsons 2007, 12).

State-building: Development of institutions which manage, protect, and advance the interests and people of the state.

Structural Causal Mechanism: refers to the physical origins like geography; an individual will select the best choice given obstacles and cannot change the physical (Parsons 2007, 12).

# REFERENCE LIST

Acemoglu, Daron, and James A. Robinson. 2012. *Why nations fail: The origins of power, prosperity, and poverty.* New York: Random House.

Barnett, Michael. 2006. Building a republican peace: Stabilizing states after war. *International Security* 30, no. 4 (Spring): 87-112.

BBC. 2012. 'Baby Doc' Duvalier returns to Haiti from exile. 17 January 2011. http://www.bbc.co.uk/news/world-11943820 (accessed 31 May 2012).

Bueno de Mesquita, Bruce, and George W. Downs. 2006. Intervention and democracy. *International Organziation* 60 (Summer): 627-649.

Caplan, Richard. 2007. Who guards the guardians?: International accountability in Bosnia. In *State-Building: Theory and Practice*, edited by Aiden Hehir and Neil Robinson, 107-124. London: Routledge.

CJA: The Center for Justice and Accountability: Bringing Human Rights Abusers to Justice. 2011. Background on Somalia. http://www.cja.org/article.php?id=436 (accessed 16 May 2012).

Chandler, David. 2007. The state-builidng dilemma: Good governance or democratic government? In *State-Building: Theory and practice*, edited by Aidan Hehir and Neil Robinson, 70-88. London: Routledge.

Chauvet, Lisa, Paul Collier, and Anke Hoeffler. 2007. *The cost of failing states and the limits to sovereignty.* Research Paper No. 2007/30, United Nations University, Helsinki: UNU-WIDER.

Chesterman, Simon. 2004. *You, the people: the United Nations, transitional adminstration, and state-building.* Oxford: Oxford University Press.

Chopra, Jarat. 2007. Building state failure in East Timor. In *State Building: Theory and Practice*, edited by Aidan Hehir and Neil Robinson, 142-166. London: Routledge.

Collier, Paul. 2011. Job creation, investment promotion, and the provision of basic service. *Prism*: 17-30.

Dahl, Robert A. 1998. *On Democracy.* New Haven: Yale University Press.

Democracy Index. 2012a. Democracy index 2010: Democracy in retreat. A report from the economist intelligence unit. http://graphics.eiu.com/PDF/ Democracy_Index_2010_web.pdf (accessed 31 May 2012).

Dixon, Gregory C. 2011. Not ever good enough for government work: Industrial democracies and nation-building. Conference paper presented 31 January 2011 at the Southern Political Science Conference.

Dobbins, James. 2006. Learning the lessons of Iraq. In *Nation-builiding: Beyond Afghanistan and Iraq*, edited by Francis Fukuyama, 218-229. Baltimore: The Johns Hopkins University Press.

Dobbins, James, John G. McGinn, Keith Crane, Seth G. Jones, Rollie Lal, and Andrew Rathmell. 2003. *America's role in nation-building: From Germany to Iraq.* Santa Monica: RAND.

East Timor Government. 2011. History of East Timor. http://www.esastimore government.com/history.htm (accessed 15 May 2012).

Elden, Stuart. 2007. Terror and territory. *Antipode*: 821-845.

ETAN. 2012. United Nations security council resolutions on East Timor (1975-1976). S/RES/384 (1975). http://etan.org/etun/Unres.htm (accessed 31 May 2012).

Entelis, John P. 2007. The unchanging politics of North Africa. *Middle East Policy* 14, no. 4 (2007): 23-41.

Epstein, David L., Robert Bates, Jack Goldstone, Ida Kristensen, and Sharyn O'Halloran. 2006. Democratic transitions. *American Journal of Political Science* 50, no. 3 (July): 551-569.

Etzioni, Amitai. 2009/2010. Bottom-up nation building. *Policy Review*, no. 158 (December/January): 51-62.

European Forum. 2012. Bosnia Herzegovina: Country update. February. Eurpoean Forum for democracy and solidarity. http://europeanforum.net/country/ bosnia_herzegovina (accessed 10 May 2012).

Ezrow, Natasha M., and Erica Frantz. State institutions and the survivial of dictatorships. *Journal of International Affairs* 65, no. 1 (Fall/Winter 2011): 1-13.

Freedom House. 2012. Freedom in the world. http://www.freedomhouse.ort/ report/freedom-world (accessed 15 May 2012).

———. 2011. Freedom in the world: Somalia. http://www.freedomhouse.ort/report/ freedom-world/2011/somalia (accessed 15 May 2012).

FRIDE (Fundación para las Relaciones Internacionales y el Dialogo Exterior). 2010. How to revitalise democracy assistance: Recipients' views. Working Paper 100 . June. www.fride.com

———. 2008. *Democracy backgrounder: Elections in Bosnia and Herzegovina.* September. www.fride.org (accessed 15 May 2012).

Fukuyama, Francis. 2006a. Guidelines for future nation-builders. In *Nation-building: Beyond Afghanistan and Iraq,* edited by Francis Fukuyama, 231-244. Balitimore: The Johns Hopikins University Press.

———. ed. 2006b. *Nation-building: Beyond Afghanistan and Iraq.* Baltimore: The Johns Hopkins University Press.

———. 2004. *State-building: Governance and world order in the 21st century.* New York: Cornell University Press.

Ghani, Ashraf, and Clare Lockhart. 2009. *Fixing failed states: A framework for rebuilding a fractured world.* New York, NY: Oxford University Press.

Gibson, Clark C., Krister Andersson, Elinor Ostrom, and Sujai Shivakumar. 2005. *The samaritan's dilemma.* Oxford: Oxford University Press.

Girard, Philippe R. 2010. Underdevelopment in Haiti. In *Nation builiding, state builiding, and economic development: Case studies and comparisons,* edited by S. C. M. Paine, 153-166. Armonk: M.E. Sharpe.

Goldsmith, Arthur A. 2008. Making the world safe for partial democracy?: Questioning the premises of democracy promotion. *International Security* 33, no. 2 (Fall): 120-147.

Haitian Pearl. 2012. History of Haiti. http://haitianpearl.org/learn/history-of-haiti/ (accessed 21 May 2012).

Hehir, Aidan, and Neil Robinson. 2007. *State-building: Theory and practice.* New York: Routledge.

Huchthausen, Peter. 2003. *America's splendid little wars: A short history of U.S. engagements from the fall of Saigon to Baghdad.* New York: Penguin Books.

ICG (International Crisis Group). 1996. Elections in Bosnia and Herzegovina. http://www.crisisgroup.org/~/media/Files/europe/balkans/bosnia-herzegovina/Bosnia%202.pdf (accessed 4 June 2012).

Kaplan, Robert. 1994. The coming anarchy. *The Atlantic Monthly* 273, no. 2 (February): 44-76.

Kaplan, Seth. 2008/2009. Fixing fragile states. *Policy Review* 152 (December/January): 63-77.

KMLA. 2004. World history at KMLA: History of Somalia, 1889-1918. http://www.zum.de/whkmla/region/eastafrica/somaliapre1889.html (accessed 16 May 2012).

Krause, Keith, and Oliver Jutersonke. 2007. Seeking out the state: fragile states and international governance. *Politibus* 42 (January): 5-12.

Mansfield, Edward D., and Jack Snyder. 2002a. Democratic transitions, institutional strength, and war. *International Organization* 56, no. 2 (Spring): 297-337.

———. 2002b. Incomplete democratization and the outbreak of military disputes. *International Studies Quarterly* 46, no. 4 (December): 529-549.

MERLN. 2012. The United States national security strategy. http://merln.ndu.edu (accessed 19 May 2012).

Mundt, Robert J. 1997. Is democracy stable? Compared to what?: A preliminary exploration. Presented at the 1997 American Political Science Association Conference. http://www.stier.net/writing/demstab/stability.htm

Nelson, Stephen, and Geoffrey Wallace. 2012. The IMF and democracy. In *Liberal iterventionism and democracy promotion*, edited by Dursun Peksen, 87-114. Lanham: Lexington Books.

Owen, John M. IV. 2002. The foreign impostion of domestic insitutions. *International Organization* 56, no. 2 (Spring): 379-409.

Paine, S.C.M., ed. 2010. *Nation building, state building, and economic development: Case studies and comparisons.* Armonk, NY: M.E.Sharpe.

Paris, Roland. 2004. *At war's end: Building peace after civil conflict.* Cambridge: Cambridge University Press.

Parsons, Craig. 2007. *How to map arguements in political science.* Oxford: Oxford University Press.

Pearson, Frederic S., and Marie Olson Lounsbery. 2012. Soft power and democratization. In *Liberal interventionism and democracy promotion*, edited by Dursun Peksen, 68-73. Lanham: Lexington Books.

Pei, Minxin, Samia Amin, and Seth Garz. 2006. The American experience. In *Nation-builidng: Beyond Afghanistan and Iraq*, edited by Francis Fukuyama, 64-85. Baltimore: The Johns Hopkins University Press.

Peksen, Dursun, ed. 2012. *Liberal intervention and democracy promotion.* Lanham, MD: Lexington Books.

Pickering, Jeffrey, and Emizet F. Kisangani. 2006. Political, economic, and social consequences of foreign military intervention. *Political Research Quarterly* 59, no. 3 (September): 363-376.

Pickering, Jeffrey, and Mark Peceny. 2006. Forging democracy at gunpoint. *International Studies Quarterly* 50: 539-559.

Proceedings of CAMDUN-1. 1991. *Building a more democratic United Nations.* Edited by Frank Barnaby. London: Frank Cass,.

Read, Anthony, and David Fisher. 1997. *The proudest day: India's long road to independence.* New York. W.W. Norton and Company.

Robinson, Neil. 2007. State-building and international poltics: The emergence of a 'new' problem and agenda. In *State-building: Theory and practice*, edited by Aidan Hehir and Neil Robinson, 1-28. London: Routledge.

Samuels, Kirsti. 2005. Sustainability and peace builiding: A key challenge. *Development in practice* 15, no. 6 (November): 728-736.

Sells, Michael A. 1996. *The bridge betrayed: Religion and genocide in Bosnia.* Berkeley: Univeristy of California Press.

Smith, Rogers M. 2003. *Stories of peoplehood: The politics and morals of political membership.* Cambridge: Cambridge University Press.

Somit, Albert, and Steven A. Peterson. 2005. *The failure of democratic nation building: Ideology meets evolution.* New York: Palgrave Macmillan.

Sutton, Francis X. 2006. Nation-building in the heyday of development ideology. In *Nation-building: Beyond Afghanistan and Iraq*, edited by Francis Fukuama, 42-63. Baltimore, MD: The Johns Hopkins University Press.

Talentino, Andrea Kathryn. 2009. Nation building or nation splitting? Political transition and the dangers of violence. *Terrorism and political violence* 21 (2009): 378-400.

————. 2004. The two faces of nation-building: Developing function and identity. *Cambridge Review of International Affairs* 17, no. 3 (October): 557-575.

Thiranagama, Sharika, and Tobias Kelly. 2010. *Traitors: Suspicion, intimacy, and the ethics of state-building.* Philadelphia: University of Pennsylvania Press.

Tusalem, Rollin F. 2012. The UN and democracy promotion. In *Liberal interventionism and democracy promotion*, edited by Dursun Peksen, 233. Lanham: Lexington Books.

von Hippel, Karin von. 2000. Democracy by force: A renewed commitment to nation building. *The Washington Quarterly* 23, no. 1 (Winter): 95-112.

Watson, Cynthia A. 2004. *Nation building: A reference handbook.* Santa Barbara: ABC CLIO.

Wilde, Ralph. 2007. Colonialism redux? Territorial administration by international organizations, colonial echoes and the legitimacy of the international. In *State-building: Theory and practice*, edited by Aidan Hehir and Neil Robinson, 29-49. London: Routledge.

Wolpert, Stanley. 2004. *A new history of India,* 7th ed. New York. Oxford University Press.

Zakaria, Fareed. 2003. *Future of freedom: Illiberal democracy home and abroad.* New York: W.W. Norton and Company.

www.ingramcontent.com/pod-product-compliance
Lightning Source LLC
Chambersburg PA
CBHW081846280526
45789CB00007B/2587